STANDING INTO DANGER

TWO HUNDRED YEARS OF LIFEBOAT SERVICE IN THE RIVER TAY AND ST ANDREWS BAY

ANDREW JEFFREY

DUNDEE BRANCH, RNLI

BY THE SAME AUTHOR

This Dangerous Menace. Dundee and the River Tay at War 1939-1945. (Mainstream 1991)

This Present Emergency. Edinburgh, the River Forth and South East Scotland in the Second World War. (Mainstream 1992)

This Time of Crisis. Glasgow, the West of Scotland and the North West Approaches in the Second World War. (Mainstream 1993)

At least 70% of the revenue from the sale of this book will support the Broughty Ferry lifeboats in the saving of lives at sea.

Front cover; RNLB Spirit of Tayside**.**
(PHOTO BY MURRAY AT PBM (COMMERCIAL) PHOTOGRAPHIC)

Back cover; *Relief inshore lifeboat* Pride of Nuneaton and Bedworth *in St Andrews Bay.*
(ROBERT BROWN)

Copyright © Andrew Jeffrey 1996

All rights reserved.

The moral right of the author has been asserted.

First published in Great Britain in 1996 by
Dundee Branch, The Royal National Lifeboat Institution,
The Lifeboat Shed, Fisher Street, Broughty Ferry, Dundee DD5 1EF. Tel: 01382 779956

ISBN 0 9527568 0 3

A catalogue record for this book is available from the British Library.

Typeset in 11 pt Times New and printed by Tayport Printers Ltd., Shanwell Court Industrial Estate, Shanwell Road, Tayport, Fife DD6 9EA. Tel; 01382 552381

STANDING INTO DANGER

Contents

Dedication

This book is dedicated to the memory of the crew of the Broughty Ferry lifeboat RNLB Mona which was lost with all hands in the early hours of Tuesday, 8 December 1959. The lifeboat foundered while responding to a call from the North Carr lightship which was adrift in St Andrews Bay.

From left; Ex-Coxswain Alex Gall, Motor Mechanic John Grieve, John Grieve jun., James Ferrier, David Anderson and Second Coxswain George Smith. (Not shown; Coxswain Ronald Grant and Bowman George Watson.)

It is also dedicated to the memory of Launchers George Sharp and Patrick Flannigan who lost their lives while launching the St Andrews lifeboat, and to a young Broughty Ferry fisherman by the name of Knight who drowned while helping to rescue the crew of the brig Fifeshire on the Gaa Sands in February 1848.

(DUNDEE BRANCH, RNLI)

Foreword

by

Brian Callison

My initial reaction, on being asked to contribute this foreword to Andrew Jeffrey's meticulously researched history encompassing two centuries of lifeboat service in the River Tay and St Andrews Bay, was to feel greatly honoured. That awareness of privilege was quickly replaced by one of concern. How, in a brief introduction, could I hope to pay adequate tribute to the former generations of local volunteers who dedicated themselves - on certain tragic occasions, sacrificed their own existences - to the often perilous, always vital business of saving life at sea? How might I give full due to the unassuming work of the officers and officials, the launchers, the committee members and the fund raisers without whose unstinting support no service could be maintained? Above all, how could I justify using superlatives which will merely embarrass those Tayside lifeboatmen of today who, even as you read this, hold themselves in all-weather readiness for the Broughty Ferry Shout?

But then I realised how eminently qualified I am to salute them without inhibition - all of them, past and present. Because I write with the authority of the consumer. Having been a twice-distressed seafarer during my own maritime-related career I can, from the casualty's point of view, express my unbounded gratitude to the men and women of the Royal National Lifeboat Institution; hopefully without causing embarrassment at all.

Neither misadventure rated worthy of inclusion on the scale by which true peril at sea is measured - apart, perhaps, from that devised by myself and my fellow crew members of the times. I mention them only to introduce the fact that the lifeboat which responded to my maiden request for assistance was the RNLB *Mona,* launched from Broughty Ferry station. Her official service return for 8 April 1957 solemnly lists the *Number of lives rescued from shipwreck by the lifeboat* as being eight. And one dog.

Less than three years later, eight members of the *Mona's* crew were to make the ultimate sacrifice in circumstances explored with great sensitivity in the narrative which follows. You will judge for yourself what calibre of men they were. What courage and fortitude they displayed by their concern for their fellow seafarers.

Yet, despite that, I can confirm that the term *hero* never appears in this history. Andrew tells me this is a calculated omission which characterises the modesty and sheer professionalism of those who continue to uphold the humanitarian traditions of the River Tay and St Andrews Bay lifeboatmen. I respect that prohibition, and I understand it.

But when I hear the wind gusting force nine in the middle of a freezing black December night or glimpse, from my comfortable window, the spume-hazed maelstrom that can sometimes mark the Tay approaches, I think of the men of the *Mona.* Of those who served before them, and of those who serve today. And my inadequacies as a writer come flooding to the surface.

Because, for the life of me, I cannot conceive of another description so fitting as the one I feel honour bound not to use.

Crossing The Bar - RNLB Spirit of Tayside

Build me straight, O worthy Master!
Staunch and strong, a goodly vessel,
That shall laugh at all disaster,
And with wave and whirlwind wrestle.

(PHOTO BY ROBERT BROWN - VERSE BY H.W. LONGFELLOW)

Chapter One

LAUNCH!

Squalls of sleet and snow hustled through the streets of Broughty Ferry, rattling angrily at the windows of the old cottages clustered around the harbour and the lifeboat shed. Almost the only people out and about on that freezing, gale-lashed Tuesday night, the 5th of December 1939, were air-raid wardens checking on the wartime blackout.

Far away in the South Atlantic, Royal Navy cruisers were hunting down the German pocket battleship *Graf Spee*. On the Western Front, the war had degenerated into a snow-bound stalemate in which French and German soldiers contented themselves with yelling insults at each other through powerful loudspeakers. Closer to home, 40 miles east of Fife Ness, Kapitanleutnant Zahn of the *U56* had torpedoed the neutral Swedish steamer *Rudolf*. Nine of the *Rudolf's* 32 crewmen died and the survivors were brought into the Tay that afternoon after spending almost 24 hours in two open boats. One of the vessels searching for the missing sailors had been the Broughty Ferry lifeboat RNLB *Mona*.

Suddenly, just after 8.00 p.m., the village streets echoed to the slamming of doors and the tramp of running feet. The word went round, 'There's a trawler on the Bell Rock. The lifeboat's going out.' Coxswain Jim Coull and his crew hurriedly pulled on oilskins, lifejackets and sou-westers as they climbed aboard the *Mona*. The doors at the bottom of the boatshed were drawn back and the lifeboatmen stared out into the darkness, just able to see the wind-whipped waves breaking close to the top of the slipway. A few terse words, the roar of engines, the shrill blast of a whistle, and the *Mona* was sliding down the slipway into her natural element.

Eighteen miles away, on the Bell Rock, the crew of the Aberdeen trawler *Quixotic* were in desperate straits. They had left Aberdeen that afternoon bound for the coaling berth at Leith before heading for the North Sea fishing grounds. Night navigation in wartime was particularly hazardous as, in addition to the dangers of being torpedoed or striking a drifting mine, every navigational beacon on the coast had been blacked out to foil enemy bombers.

Skipper William Gardiner and his crew were peering into the inky blackness, keeping a sharp lookout for the Bell Rock Lighthouse that marked the dreaded Inchcape Reef. Suddenly, they saw breakers ahead. The engine was put full astern and the wheel hard over, but it was too late. Helpless before the northerly gale, *Quixotic* crashed onto the north side of the reef just 30 feet from the base of the lighthouse.

Instantly, the rhythmic beat of the steam engine gave way to the tortured grinding and screaming of steel plate against rock. *Quixotic* was 41 years old and her hull could take little of this sort of punishment. The sea was soon pouring into her and she settled until she lay with a steep list to port and her stern awash. Icy waves burst over her decks as Skipper Gardiner and his crew struggled forward to the bows where they burned their clothing, blankets, even their boots in an effort to attract attention.

The trawlermen could see the tower of the lighthouse looming over them. Faintly over the roaring of the sea, they could hear shouts as the lightkeepers tried to throw a line across to the stricken trawler. Coastguards at Carnoustie and Fife Ness were alerted by a radio message from the lighthouse and, moments later, the telephone began to ring in Coxswain Coull's Broughty Ferry home. At 8.17 p.m., less than twenty minutes after the *Quixotic* struck, the *Mona* was on her way to the rescue.

Buddon Ness light was switched on for a few moments to help the lifeboat find her way through the treacherous sandbars at the entrance to the River Tay. As she crossed the open water between the fairway buoy and the Bell Rock, the *Mona's* crew could see the lights of the Arbroath lifeboat *John and William Mudie* as she too answered the distress call. The Arbroath lifeboat was first to reach the stranded trawler and fired a rocket line across her only for this to foul and carry away. A naval patrol boat and the Arbroath lifeboat then switched on their searchlights to help the *Mona* close the wreck. Unable to get alongside the *Quixotic*'s leeward side due to rocks, Coxswain Coull anchored the lifeboat to windward and used the anchor cable to veer down, stern first, until a grapnel could be thrown aboard the trawler.

Huge waves broke across the *Mona* and only seamanship of the highest order saved her from a similar fate to that of the trawler. The lifeboat was bucking and rearing on the end of her anchor warp such that one minute her crew were gazing at the trawler's keel, the next minute they could see clear across her deck. The sea crashed against rocks desperately close to the lifeboat's stern and, in the troughs, she had just two feet of water under her keel. Lifeboatman Willie Findlay suffered bruised ribs when he was almost swept overboard.

The rescued crew of the Quixotic *in the Sailor's Home, Dundee.*
(ARBROATH HERALD)

The Aberdeen steam trawler Quixotic *impaled on the reef next to the Bell Rock lighthouse. This photograph, taken after the gale had subsided, does little to convey the dangers faced by the crew of the* Mona *as they closed the wreck.*
(ARBROATH GUIDE)

Hauling alternately on either the anchor cable or the grapnel line and skilful juggling of the engine controls brought the lifeboat repeatedly alongside the *Quixotic* and the frozen trawlermen were able to jump across one by one. Finally, after more than half an hour in this perilous position, all nine of the trawler's sodden and numb crew were safely aboard the *Mona* and she set sail for home. Hot baths and dry clothing had been made ready in St James' Hall when the nine survivors were landed at Broughty Ferry at 1.00 a.m. All had sustained cut feet and minor head wounds, but only Second Engineer John Pirrie was detained in Dundee Royal Infirmary suffering from shock. Andrew Innes, the mate of the *Quixotic*, was full of praise for the extraordinary seamanship displayed by the Broughty Ferry lifeboatmen.

The scratched and dented *Mona* was rehoused and refuelled. She was launched for the third time in four days just 36 hours later when the Icelandic trawler *Skallagrimur* was reported in distress 17 miles south east of Fife Ness. No trace was ever found of the trawler or her crew.

Dundee Branch of the RNLI held their Annual General Meeting in Dundee City Chambers at 2.30 p.m. on Friday, 10 May 1940. The meeting was a somewhat hurried affair as, that very morning, Hitler had launched his *blitzkreig* of France, Belgium and the Low Countries. Branch President Ralph Cowper asked Lady Barrie to present Coxswain Coull with an RNLI silver medal and Motor Mechanic Johnny Grieve and Second Coxswain George Smith with bronze medals for their courage and skill during the *Quixotic* service. She also presented the Thanks of the Institution on Vellum to crewmen Sam Craig, George Watson, George Gall, Willie Findlay and Robert Smith.

Almost 20 years to the day after the *Quixotic* service, the *Mona* was to be in the news again, this time in truly tragic circumstances. The North Carr lightship was reported adrift in St Andrews Bay in the early hours of Tuesday, 8 December 1959, in one of the worst gales to hit the east coast for many years. Having been launched to her aid, the *Mona* was discovered at daybreak on Buddon Sands near Carnoustie. In and around her were the bodies of seven of her eight crew, among them George Smith, Johnny Grieve and his 22-year-old son John.

The approaches to the River Tay are widely acknowledged as being among the most dangerous waters anywhere on the British coast. Sailing ships driven before easterly winds into the encircling arms of St Andrews Bay, were regularly hurled onto the rocky shore of Fife between St Andrews and Fife Ness. Vessels that made the Tay approaches often missed the buoys that marked the narrow entrance to the navigable channel and ran onto the Abertay or Gaa Sands.

Returning to station – RNLB Mona
(SUSAN HUGHAN)

On a fine, calm day, these banks of golden sand dotted with sunbathing seals can appear deceptively benign. In reality, they are the graves of countless ships and men. The landsman thinks of sand as a soft, warm substance so much a part of hot summer days spent improving a tan. For the seaman, however, sandbanks such as those at the entrance to the Tay are particularly menacing. Impregnated with round boulders, they are iron hard and just touching the edge of one was enough to rip the bottom out of a wooden sailing ship.

The banks, and the sandbar which crosses the navigable channel between them, make this a fearsome place in bad weather, particularly when an easterly gale meets a fast-running ebb tide flowing out of the river. Ships in the narrow channel are tossed around mercilessly in a maelstrom of huge, confused seas created by the combination of wind, tide and shoal water. To port and starboard, lines of white, crashing breakers mark the position of the sandbanks, ever-ready to devour the unwary.

Man had been harvesting rich shoals of fish in St Andrews Bay since the beginning of time but an entirely new phenomenon, industrialisation, came with the early years of the 19th century. A landmark was reached on 4 April 1814 when, with a flurry of paddles and trailing a cloud of black smoke, the little green and yellow steamer *Tay* crept out of Dundee Harbour for the first time and set sail for Perth. Painfully slow and inefficient she might have been, but the *Tay* was symbolic of the massive leap forward in technology that transformed Dundee into a world-ranking industrial centre. As industrialisation accelerated, so more and more vessels used the River Tay and an ever greater number of ships found themselves in peril.

Lifeboats have stood guard over St Andrews Bay and the entrance to the River Tay for almost two centuries since the first boat was stationed at St Andrews in January 1802. Lifeboat stations have, at various times, been established at Broughty Ferry, Buddon Ness, St Andrews, Boarhills, Crail (Fife Ness) and Magdalen Green in Dundee. Often in the most appalling conditions, the volunteer lifeboatmen who manned these boats have saved more than 800 lives. On occasion, they have given their own lives in attempting to save the lives of others.

This is their story.

Chapter Two

THE INSTRUMENTS OF OUR DELIVERANCE

Cold, grey light filtered weakly through the stained-glass windows of the College Church, St Andrews. Snow showers and violent gusts of wind had left those gathered for the Induction of the new Principal of the United Colleges, James Playfair, looking cold and bedraggled. It was Friday, 5 January 1800, and Britain was at war with France. Prime Minister William Pitt had just rejected a peace offer from Napoleon Bonaparte, income tax was being levied for the first time to help pay for the war and, in Ireland, Catholics were rioting against union with Britain.

The six foot four inch figure of 19 year-old divinity student and athlete John Honey towered over the rest of the congregation in the College Church. During the service, Dr John Adamson, Professor of Civil History, whispered urgently to him that a ship was ashore on the East Sands. As the sonorous Latin ceremonial battled against the January storm, Adamson hissed that Honey's skills as a swimmer were urgently required.

At the beach, Honey found a large crowd watching the wreck of the brig *Janet* of Macduff. Her crew had tried to float a line ashore and one man, in a desperate effort to catch it, had rushed into the breakers only to be thrown ashore gasping for breath. The line was carried away by a cross current and experienced seamen said that nothing more could be done.

John Honey was not so easily discouraged. He stripped off, tied a rope round his waist and, with a clasp knife held between his teeth, dashed into the breakers. At first he appeared to be swimming strongly but those paying out the rope did not let out enough slack. Honey swam back to the shore, told his helpers to give him more rope, and dived once more into the icy sea. Again, the rope was held too tightly so he took the knife from his teeth, cut it, and swam on. Climbing aboard the wreck, he returned to the beach with another rope, then went back and forward to assist the master and his four crew ashore.

John Honey, the survivors and many of the spectators repaired to a nearby inn to warm up. Later, the intrepid rescuer was publicly entertained by the St Andrews magistrates and presented with a silver cup by the Earl of Kellie. He was also awarded the silver medal of the Royal Humane Society. John Honey died, aged just 32, in 1814.

Among the crowd at the East Sands on that bitterly cold Friday afternoon had been St Andrews magistrate and canvas manufacturer Cathcart Dempster and it was John Honey's daring that inspired him to institute a public subscription towards the purchase of a lifeboat. The first purpose-built lifeboat had been constructed for the Tyne Lifeboat Society by South Shields boatbuilder Henry Greathead in 1789, and it was to Greathead that Cathcart Dempster and the magistrates of St Andrews turned for their lifeboat. Lloyds of London contributed towards the cost of a number of the early lifeboats, including that at St Andrews, in the hope that their investment would help reduce insurance claims arising from shipwreck.

Greathead's *Original* lifeboat was 30 feet ten inches long, double-ended and was propelled by ten oarsmen. The first Greathead *Originals* were neither self-righting nor self-bailing but were fitted with thick layers of cork to provide buoyancy. It was these layers of cork that led to the St Andrews boat being christened the *Cork Lifeboat*.

The *Edinburgh Courant* gives an account of the first trials of the St Andrews lifeboat in a report dated Tuesday, 12 January 1802;

> Through the exertions of Dean of Guild Cathcart Dempster, Almighty God has been pleased to bless this part of the coast with an excellent lifeboat built by the ingenious Mr Greathead. In the tempestuous weather of last week, we made two trials of her performance which answered the most sanguine expectations. The early motion with which she mounted and descended the proudest billows, and cast herself upon the fiercest breakers, excited the utmost interest and admiration. In the second trial, in a great measure at the mercy of the waves, under God she landed on the beach without injury to herself or danger to the crew, and thus afforded the numerous spectators on the shore a pleasing pledge of her future usefulness, when God, in the more awful visitations of his providence, shall require her services in saving the lives of any of our fellow creatures.

The *Cork Lifeboat* was launched from the Swilcan Burn for her only effective service as breakers thundered into St Andrews Bay before an easterly gale on 10 January 1803. On seeing the conditions, local fishermen were reluctant to man her until Cathcart Dempster, Captain David Stewart and a Major Horsburgh volunteered their services. All twelve of the crew of the brig *Meanwell* of Scarborough were landed safely.

Scotland's first lifeboat had been stationed at Montrose in September 1801. The St Andrews boat was second in January 1802 and was followed by Ayr and Aberdeen by January 1803. Arbroath lifeboat was established on 12 March 1803, two months after the *Meanwell* service. Fraserburgh, Ardrossan and Dunbar came next between 1806 and 1808.

What became known as 'The Long Storm' began on 12 January 1823 and lasted for 12 days. It returned with renewed ferocity on Saturday, 1 February, when the brig *Jean* of Arundel was seen in distress off St Andrews. From the Kirkhill, through a curtain of snow, John Wilson saw the faint glow of her stern light as she was driven past the castle onto the West Sands. Her crew, seven men and a boy, were able to wade ashore as the tide receded. A crowd had gathered the following morning to salvage her cargo of timber when, suddenly, the snow lifted to reveal another large brig in the breakers some way out on the bar of the Eden.

The old *Cork Lifeboat* was still in her boatshed on the East Bents but was in no fit state to be used. Neglected since the *Meanwell* service in 1803, she had fallen into disrepair. Nobody had bothered to repair a hole in the roof of the boatshed and, subsequently, part of one wall collapsed. Local youngsters climbed in to steal her cork for use as creel floats and the boat became useless. The *Craignoon*, a former Bressay fishing yawl owned by innkeeper Tam Wemyss and Captain Robert Philp, was lying in the harbour. *Craignoon* was dragged sledge-like through the snow-covered streets and across the links to the mouth of the Eden from where she made two trips to the 250 ton brig *Itinerant* and took off five survivors. One man remained but the *Craignoon*'s exhausted crew were unable to get alongside at the third attempt and returned to the beach empty-handed. A fresh crew took off the last survivor.

Meanwhile, as *Craignoon* was being hauled out after her final trip to the *Itinerant,* the *John and Sarah* of Woodbridge was drifting into the shoal water off the Eden. She had been lying at anchor near the Tay fairway buoy for two days in appalling weather and, when she began to founder, her crew were presented with a stark choice; either sink where they were, or attempt to run their ship onto the beach. *Craignoon* went out again and took off three of the *John and Sarah*'s crew. The other three refused to leave until they had collected their personal belongings, a decision that was to cost them their lives as, despite making six more attempts, *Craignoon* was unable to get alongside the wreck.*

The rescues carried out by the *Craignoon* led to the ordering of a replacement for the old *Cork Lifeboat*. The new St Andrews lifeboat was towed round from her Tyneside builders in September 1824 by coal merchant John Black in his brig *Ocean*. Twenty seven feet long and built of copper fastened oak, she had 16 airtight compartments, two long side compartments filled with cork chips and five copper relieving tubes, and was designed locally for use as a surf boat on the East and West Sands. On arrival, she was lowered into the harbour keel uppermost to demonstrate her self-righting capabilities and turned upright without difficulty.

The new boat, christened the *Volunteer Lifeboat,* carried out her first service in 1825 when the waterlogged smack *Trafulgin* was trapped in St Andrews Bay during a storm. Lt Goodchild RN, the Senior Coastguard at St Andrews, and six of his staff formed the nucleus of the *Volunteer Lifeboat*'s crew. Goodchild had the lifeboat taken from her boatshed next to the Swilcan Bridge, dragged across the links and launched at the mouth of the burn. Almost immediately, she was struck by a heavy sea that burst some of her copper relieving tubes.

More than 58 years later, in 1883, volunteer crew member Aleck Wilson could still recall

---

* One of those manning the *Craignoon* that day was George Skinners, a coasting skipper better known as 'Scotch Geordie'. Once sheepskins had been nailed over the worst of her leaks, the *Itinerant* was refloated and repaired. Scotch Geordie was given command of her and used to announce his arrival in the Tyne with a lusty tune on his bagpipes.

this, the *Volunteer Lifeboat*'s first service. 'Man, I was intil her the first time she was aff. I was only 18 years old at the time. I mind I was pullin' ane o' the bow oars when a sea struck her that burst her tubes and sent my neebor bow-oarsman, ane o' the coastguard, richt up in the air aboot twel' fit, and he fell doon again nearly in the same place in the bow o' the boat.'

Goodchild put men aboard the *Trafulgin* and brought both the smack and her crew safely into harbour. The master of the *Trafulgin* insisted on showing his appreciation in the bar of Wallace's Hotel and, by the time he left, the amiable Goodchild was described as 'half seas over.' He had the misfortune to run into Captain Randal, the senior coastguard in Fife, and was promptly sacked. His replacement, Lt Henry Cox RN, carried out the first of his many services as coxswain of the *Volunteer Lifeboat* in 1826. On that occasion, the boat rescued two brothers called Dorrit, owners of the Tayport fishing sloop *Friends* that had foundered off the mouth of the Eden in bad weather.

Coal was the black life-blood of the industrial revolution. Prior to the advent of railways and with the road network still primitive, the only way to move it around the country was by sea. The little schooner *Fancy* was approaching the Tay on 9 February 1828 with a cargo of coal from Newcastle. Captain Ritchie peered through showers of driving snow, searching desperately for the Buddon Ness Lights. When placed in line, these indicated to mariners that they were safely in the first leg of the Tay channel.

John Marr, the 'Ingenious Marriner', published his first chart of the east coast of Scotland in 1680. This showed a small light on the point at 'Bottanais' and a 'Great Light' further inland, both fire beacons thought to date from before 1600. The first sailing directions for the River Tay were contained in John Adair's *Description of the Sea-Coast, etc, of Scotland* published in 1703. As late as 1755 the Buddon lights were still the only beacons on the entire east coast of Scotland apart from the fire beacon on Isle of May that dated from 1636.

On the *Fancy,* Captain Ritchie had been completely blinded by the snowstorm and was being pushed ever further into danger by an easterly gale. He dropped anchor but this dragged and, completely helpless, he was driven onto the Elbow End sandbank. Two of his crew were washed overboard and the remaining three spent 12 hours clinging to the rigging of their sunken ship before being rescued by fishermen. For his part in the rescue, Broughty Ferry fisherman Dan Kidd was awarded the silver medal of the Royal National Institution for the Preservation of Life from Shipwreck.

This Institution, later the Royal National Lifeboat Institution, was formed in the City of London Tavern on 12 February 1824 following a public appeal made by former adventurer and soldier Sir William Hillary. Entitled *An Appeal to the British Nation on the Humanity and Policy of forming a National Institution for the Preservation of Lives and Property from Shipwreck,* it resulted from Hillary's own rescue efforts during a series of wrecks near his Isle of Man home in 1822.

Dundee in the late 1820s was a city growing prosperous on the linen trade. A commercial gas company formed in 1826 built the city's first gas works in Peep o' Day Lane and provided the first public lighting service. A thrice-daily coaching service between the Eagle Inn, Broughty Ferry, and Dundee began in 1826. In the summer of 1828, the Kirk Session of Dundee attempted, unsuccessfully, to have the master of the first Sunday excursion steamer between the city and Broughty Ferry prosecuted for 'profanation of the Sabbath'. A regular steamer service offering four trips each way daily was not established until 1832.

In 1815, at the time of the Battle of Waterloo, Dundee Harbour consisted of two crude rubble breakwaters and a small tidal basin. It was run by town councillors who doggedly refused to spend money on improvements and the facility was hopelessly inadequate for the needs of a burgeoning industrial city. Things did begin to improve when management of the harbour was transferred to commissioners and Thomas Telford was instructed to undertake improvement works including the construction of King William IV Dock and Earl Grey Dock. In 1830, however, with the harbour improvements almost complete, the Town Council saw their chance and attempted to wrest control of the new facilities back from the Harbour Commission. They were unsuccessful and Dundee Harbour Trust was formed, the body which managed the port for over 130 years.

A series of gales towards the end of 1829 was to lead directly to the establishment of the first River Tay lifeboat. On 3 August the Tay ferry steamer *Union* broke her paddleshaft while crossing from Newport and anchored in the river. The tender used to land her passengers was driven down river to Carolina Port by a strong westerly breeze. There the passengers disembarked and four boatmen, who volunteered to take their luggage to the Craig Pier, drowned when their boat capsized near the Beacon Rock.

In another storm that autumn, a large, coal-laden brig was driven into St Andrews Bay, finally coming to her anchor perilously close to the banks at the entrance to the Tay. Try as they might, Lt Cox and his crew could not get the *Volunteer Lifeboat* through the rollers on the West Sands until the following morning. They got aboard the brig to find that her anchor cable had parted. There was no sign of her crew of nine who had clearly drowned while attempting to abandon ship during the night. Cox worked the brig into the Tay and up to Dundee.

Another brig, the *Childe Harold* of Dundee, was inbound from St Petersburg in an easterly gale on the night of Tuesday, 24 November 1829. Captain Alexander Swap got into difficulties while rounding the Elbow End and struck the bank at about 11.00 p.m. As the brig sank, her crew hurriedly made a raft of spars and barrels and landed at Buddon, all except for a young lad named Ross who was drowned. Broughty Ferry fisherman David Knight found the exhausted, frozen seamen on Buddon Sands the following morning. One of them, described as 'a black man', held onto the raft with what was termed a 'death grip'. Captain Swap survived the wreck of his ship only to die four days later when the *Childe Harold*'s mast fell on him during an attempt to salvage her cargo.

It would appear that the wreck of the *Childe Harold* and the rescue of her crew at last motivated a number of shipowners and shipmasters to take action. Two weeks later, on Thursday, 3 December 1829, the following item appeared in the *Dundee, Perth and Cupar Advertiser;*

> We have much satisfaction in stating that at a meeting of the Tay Steam Packet Co., held yesterday, a number of Gentlemen formed themselves into a committee for procuring, by subscription, what has long been a desideration here - a life boat. The subscription was commenced and will, we trust, be speedily filled up.

A week later, the *Advertiser*'s 'Local Intelligence' included the news that the lifeboat committee had lodged subscription papers in all the Dundee Banks and in the Shore Dues Office in the harbour. Subscription papers were also to be had from James Chalmers' bookshop and printing business in Castle Street, Dundee. Widely credited with the invention of the postage stamp in August 1834, Chalmers was also a harbour trustee, a member of the first lifeboat committee and, from 1837 to 1840, Dundee Town Treasurer.

Another leading figure in the lifeboat committee was Alex Martin, the Boxmaster of the Fraternity of Masters and Seamen. The Fraternity was one of the ancient Guildry and Trades of Dundee, having received formal recognition in 1556. For the first 130 years of its existence, it was primarily a benefit society paying out pensions to retired seamen. In 1687 it was made responsible for all of the buoyage and lighting in the River Tay, collecting a levy on ships using the river. In former days, the money raised was kept in 'The Box' and was the responsibility of the boxmaster elected annually from the membership.

On 15 December 1829, two weeks after the AGM of the Tay Steam Packet Co., the Fraternity authorised Boxmaster Alex Martin, 'To subscribe £20 for the purpose of procuring a lifeboat for the Tay.' Two days later, the *Advertiser* reported;

> Although the public generally were asked to contribute, only in the last two or three days has progress been made. Yesterday forenoon upwards of £80 had been raised, and as none of the Shipping Companies and but few of the principal Shipowners or Merchants had been applied to for their contributions, there was reason to hope that a sum will be raised as will be sufficient not only to purchase the boat, but to keep it in repair and to supply occasional rewards to those who use it dexterously in the preservation of life.

On the strength of the first £80 and promises of further donations, the committee ordered a boat from Robson's of South Shields. The *Advertiser* for 4 November 1830 contains the following notice to mariners;

> Shipmasters frequenting the River Tay are hereby informed that the LIFE BOAT is now complete and deposited in a house built for the purpose south of the Lights of Tay, and that the key of the boat house is in the possession of the keeper of the above Lights.
> The Light keeper has instructions to use every exertion to collect a crew for manning the boat and to render every other possible assistance in cases of casualty.
>
> Sgd. Alex Martin.
> Boxmaster Seamen's Fraternity.
> PS There are still several of those who subscribed for the purpose of procuring the Life Boat who have not yet paid their subscriptions, some of whom cannot easily be found; it is therefore requested that they will call or order payment to be made to Mr Chalmers, bookseller, without delay.
> *Dundee October 25 1830.*

Built to a modified Greathead design known as the 'North Country' type, the new lifeboat was 30 feet long and cost £130. She carried a crew of 12 pulling oarsmen, two steering oarsmen and up to 25 survivors. The boatshed and slipway constructed for her at Buddon Ness cost a further £206.

A German schooner was seen struggling in St Andrews Bay in a gale late on 30 September 1831. The worst was feared for her crew when the wind increased during the night and heavy, driving rain began to fall. At daybreak, it was discovered that the schooner had grounded near the mouth of the Eden and was being pounded mercilessly by huge waves. With great difficulty, the *Volunteer Lifeboat* was launched from the West Sands at 8.30 a.m. and, as one observer wrote, 'the men were brought ashore much wasted.' The schooner broke up a few minutes after her crew were rescued and her cargo of Fraserburgh herring was washed ashore.

Launching a lifeboat across the open beach at St Andrews, particularly in bad weather, was no easy matter. The boat had first to be taken across the links to the mouth of the Swilcan Burn. More often than not, a strong easterly gale was blowing straight up the West Sands. The coxswain had to decide which of the incoming breakers would be big enough, but not too big, to carry the lifeboat out to sea. Once he had given the order to launch, there could be no turning back. The launchers, men and women alike standing up to their necks in freezing water, had to react immediately by heaving on the ropes that hauled the boat off her carriage. A moment's hesitation could see the boat capsized and many of her crew drowned. Finally, the crew had to be both disciplined and strong so that all ten oars struck the water at exactly the same moment with sufficient power to pull the boat through the surf into clear water.

Stationing the River Tay lifeboat at Buddon Ness placed her as close as possible to the sandbanks where she was likely to be most needed, but there was one drawback; it placed the boat some considerable distance from the nearest source of a crew. There were fishermen three miles away at Westhaven but the majority of the crew would have to be drawn from Broughty Ferry, some six miles distant. The only way to reach the lifeboat in either case was on foot.

It was also discovered that a lifeboat stationed at Buddon Ness was both out of sight and out of mind. There are no records of her having been used in anger before mid-September 1835 when Fraternity Boxmaster William Nicoll reported that he had removed the lifeboat to Dundee, 'In a sinking state.' Ten days later, on Friday, 25 September, the Dundee Advertiser carried the following intimation;

> A General Meeting of Subscribers, Shipowners, Shipmasters and Others, interested in the maintenance of a Life Boat for the River Tay to be held in Campbell's Hall on Wednesday next, the 30th, at twelve o'clock noon, to take into consideration the necessary repairs for the boat and the propriety of her station, and future management &c.
> *Sgd S Robertson Secy., Shore Dues Office, Dundee. September 24, 1835.*

Many advocated stationing the boat near her first crew at Broughty Ferry, from where she could be rowed down river to the banks, even though this would place her at least six miles from where she was most needed. But reaching the banks would be impossible against a flooding tide and easterly gale. On the strong recommendation of the Fraternity of Masters and Seamen, and despite its manifest disadvantages, Buddon Ness station was retained as the only practical option.

Four days after this meeting, on the morning of Sunday, 4 October 1835, Captain James Caithness sailed from Dundee bound for Glasgow with a valuable cargo of bale goods in the Dundee, Perth & London (D.P.&L.) line schooner *Tid*. The wind was blowing hard from the north, making the *Tid*'s passage down river very difficult and, while tacking to clear the Elbow End, she was caught in irons and driven down onto the bank. Immediately she struck, Caithness looked down into the cabin and could see water already flooding in. He only had time to save his pocket watch before he and his crew of five had to jump aboard their small boat.

Beach Crescent, Broughty Ferry, in 1832 by local artist Alexander Smith. Among the worthies illustrated are village bellman Davy Duncan and, at right, facing the artist in white duck trousers, with his telescope under his arm, Senior Coastguard Lieutenant Peter Stark R.N. Stark was the first coxswain of the Buddon Ness lifeboat and one of the earliest recipients of the gold medal of the RNLI.
The castle, then in ruins, was used as a coastguard look-out. The isthmus between the castle and the village was, for a time, a small shipyard. It was subsequently redeveloped into a harbour for the rail ferries that carried wagons between Broughty Ferry and Tayport prior to the building of the first Tay Bridge.
(DUNDEE ART GALLERIES AND MUSEUMS)

The *Tid*'s crew were blown towards St Andrews and were seen a short distance offshore waving their hats to attract attention as dusk fell. Henry Cox knew they were in imminent danger of being driven ashore and drowned. Calling his crew together, he took a fishing yawl from the East Sands and brought the *Tid*'s crew safely ashore at 7.00 p.m. For this particularly dangerous rescue in bad weather, Cox was awarded one of the first gold medals struck by the RNLI. His second in command, Coastguardsman Robert Fulton, was awarded a silver medal.

Repairs to the Buddon lifeboat had been completed and she was back on station one month later. At midday on Friday, 6 November 1835, the small schooner *Industry,* inbound for Dundee with a cargo of coal, was wrecked on the Gaa Sands. The wreck was seen by fishermen at Westhaven who immediately set out to man the lifeboat. What apparently happened next was described in a letter to the *Dundee Advertiser;*

Sir;- Through the medium of your journal, I beg to call the attention of subscribers to the safety life-boat stationed at the Lights of Tay, as to the propriety of its situation. If the use of such boats is to render prompt assistance to vessels in distress (when the loss of half an hour may prove fatal to life), I would then ask, how can this be achieved by having the boat in a place five [sic] miles distant of the West Haven, the nearest place where she can be manned? And also, in not appointing one who shall take the management of her when the occasion demands. The last time, or among the last times it was required, an affray took place between the second in command of the coastguard stationed at West Haven and some of the fishermen, which of them should take command of the boat; the loss of an hour was thereby occasioned, and, by such a delay, only one life was saved from a watery grave.

HUMANITAS

The sole survivor from the *Industry* was almost unconscious when brought ashore at Buddon but lightkeeper John Macartney had already sent for the doctor from Carnoustie and he soon recovered. This was the first known lifesaving service for the Buddon lifeboat.

Flax, the raw material used in linen manufacture, was being imported in large quantities from the Baltic, in particular the Russian marshes around St Petersburg. The Dundee brig *Mary*, inbound with flax from the Baltic on Boxing Day 1836, attempted to enter the river against a strong westerly wind and lost her course. Coastguards at both Westhaven and St Andrews watched her strike the Abertay Sands at 11.30 a.m. For two hours, Captain Mackenzie and his crew of seven could be seen clinging to the rigging of the sunken brig, yet no help came.

Henry Cox's opposite number as senior coastguard at Broughty Ferry was Lt Peter Stark RN. Stark attempted to raise a crew to man the lifeboat but, of the 75 fishermen in Broughty Ferry, only two, Alexander Lawrence and Charles Paul, would volunteer. They set off for Buddon by road with Stark's head boatman John Hughes. Stark, meanwhile, went out to the steam packet *Forfarshire* that was lying stormbound off Broughty Ferry. He knew that, without the help of a steamer, the lifeboat would be unable to close the wrecked brig.

Captain James Kidd got the *Forfarshire* under way as soon as possible but the *Mary* broke up before they were even half way down river to her. The rescuers found only clothing and personal effects floating among bales of flax and part of the brig's stern bearing a nameboard inscribed *Mary*.

The *Dundee Chronicle*, published by James Chalmers, commented;

In giving particulars of this melancholy event, it is painful to be obliged to notice the conduct of the Broughty Ferry fishermen, only two of whom could be prevailed upon to accompany the Head Boatman of the Preventive Service to take charge of the life boat; and, as only one individual made his appearance from Westhaven, the consequence was that, although the vessel had not broken up so speedily, there was no crew to man the life boat for the purpose of attempting to rescue the unfortunate sufferers.

Characteristically, the *Dundee Advertiser* was more robust, thundering;

The life boat establishment appears altogether defective. The boat itself is placed in a very improper situation and there is no crew attached to it; so that when an emergency occurs it is unavailable.

Why had so few men been prepared to volunteer for the lifeboat? A clue might be found in the story of the *Margaret* which went ashore near Tayport while inbound from Riga with a cargo of flax in 1831. She floated free with the tide a few hours later but, in the interim, not a single fisherman had been prepared to go anywhere near her.

Cholera, the terrible new disease from the east, had begun to make its presence felt by 1830. It was widely believed that it was being carried by the 20 or 30 flax ships arriving in the Tay every month from the Baltic. Guarded by HMS *Sybille*, a 48 gun frigate captured from the French during the Napoleonic Wars, a quarantine anchorage for ships awaiting medical clearance was organised off what is now West Ferry. A lazaretto was set up on the present-day dinghy park and here, in two specially constructed sheds, flax cargoes were landed and aired before being allowed into Dundee. As the disease took hold in other ports, so arrivals from there were quarantined; all vessels from Sunderland were quarantined from November 1831.

Despite the precautions, cholera flourished in overcrowded, insanitary Dundee and was not totally eradicated until the end of the nineteenth century. The first two deaths occurred on 27 April 1832 and, by mid-September that year, 398 cases had been recorded. The melancholy, daily progress of the hearse from the isolation hospital in what is now Whitehall Crescent up Burial Wynd, now Barrack Street, was a grim sight. Around 500 Dundonians died of the disease in the city during the 1832 epidemic and a further 542 people succumbed in August 1849 alone. To add to the misery, there were typhus epidemics in 1837 and 1847.

The debacle surrounding the loss of the *Mary* led the River Tay Lifeboat Society to convene an extraordinary general meeting. Little of substance appears to have come out of a poorly attended meeting at which much of the discussion centred on the society's chronic financial problems. Harbourmaster John Smart said afterwards, 'It is true that we have a lifeboat, but it is isolated, as you might say, from all living beings - no one nearer than two miles except the lighthouse keeper and his assistant. It is a perfect mockery to have a lifeboat without a crew.' He suggested that a powerful steamer should be stationed at Broughty Ferry and kept with steam up during gales. She could pay her way by doubling as a pilot cutter and tug. Smart's proposal was ignored, indeed the River Tay would not have its first steam pilot cutter for another 80 years.

The cholera issue surfaced again two weeks after the society meeting. The 260 ton Russian barque *St Neil* was inbound for Dundee in an easterly gale on Saturday, 31 January 1837. At about 6.00 p.m., Buddon lightkeeper John Macartney saw that she had gone too far west and was in imminent danger of running onto the Abertay Sands. He sent a message to Broughty Ferry but, again, Peter Stark had the greatest difficulty in mustering a crew. He did manage to get three pilots, one retired seaman who was by then a publican, and some lads aged between 16 and 20.

Stark and his crew set out to walk the six miles to the lifeboat shed at Buddon Ness. Two of the youngsters dropped out on the way or, as the *Dundee Chronicle* rather uncharitably put it, 'sneaked off after screwing up their courage as far as Monifieth.' On arriving at the boatshed, the crew had first to spend almost two hours clearing the slipway of snow and sand before they could launch at about midnight.

Despite the fact that his ship was making a good deal of water, the master of the *St Neil* refused all offers of assistance. Stark stood by until the tide receded and she was left high and dry on the bank then took his cold, tired crew back to Buddon for a rest. The lifeboatmen rowed back to the *St Neil* that afternoon, but still the answer was 'niet'. Stark put one of his crew, fisherman and pilot Charles Paul, aboard in case the Russian floated free at high tide, then he and his crew returned ashore, rehoused the boat and went home. The Russians did later leave their ship which was sold as a wreck.

Again, the reluctance of the Broughty fishermen to man the lifeboat attracted much hostile criticism. The *Dundee Advertiser* declared that, 'No lifeboat ever went to sea more poorly manned,' and went on to say that the behaviour of the Broughty fishermen who held back was, 'at once craven-like and curious.' Any judgement of the actions of people 160 years ago is, however, flawed by a late 20th century perspective. Cholera was an invisible killer for which there was no cure, so perhaps the fears of the fishermen are understandable.

There was no risk of cholera when the wreck of the sloop *Two Sisters* of Kirkcaldy was spotted on the banks at 4.30 a.m. on Saturday, 8 April 1837. Peter Stark had no difficulty in getting a crew together and the lifeboat reached the wreck of the *Two Sisters* in the nick of time as her crew were more dead than alive. Stark had a particularly difficult task in getting the three survivors out of the rigging as huge seas threatened to bring the lifeboat crashing down on top of the sunken sloop. For this rescue, Peter Stark was awarded a silver medal by the RNLI. Coastguardsman Craig and the rest of the lifeboat crew were awarded 10/- (50p) each.

Despite this success, it was clear that all was not well with the management of the lifeboat. Trade on the River Tay was increasing every year and the annual general meeting of the lifeboat society held on Monday, 5 June 1837 was an occasion for much plain speaking. William Just, manager of the Dundee Perth & London (D.P.&L.) shipping line, reported that after one recent gale, he had found the slipway and boatshed at Buddon blocked by drifting sand. He said that it would have taken 20 men four hours just to dig the lifeboat out.

Once again, the difficulty of manning a boat stationed so far from the nearest source of a crew was the subject of heated debate. The Westhaven men tried to suggest that the three mile walk to the boatshed made them more ready for sea but the reality was that most crews were exhausted by the time they had reached Buddon Ness and launched the boat. A suggestion that a carriage should be provided to take men from Broughty Ferry to Buddon was ridiculed on account of the terrain. The society was, however, completely reorganised with Lord Panmure as president, shipowner Patrick Just as secretary and Shore Dues Collector Simon Robertson as treasurer. Peter Stark was formally appointed coxswain and it was agreed that the crew should be paid a bounty of one guinea (£1.05) for manning the lifeboat and a further £1 if lives were saved. Membership subscriptions were instituted and, through the Fraternity of Masters and Seamen, a small levy to help pay for the lifeboat was made on shipping using the river.

The society also decided that, for ease of launching, the Buddon Ness lifeboat should lie afloat on a mooring. Two small boarding boats were, from then on, kept in the boatshed at the lighthouse. To speed up the manning of the Buddon lifeboat, a system of signals was instituted between the lighthouse, the coastguard signal station at Broughty Castle and the harbour office at the Earl Grey Dock. An ensign with the union downmost indicated that a vessel was on the banks and a crew was required. Other day signals included a variety of flags either reversed or flown in particular manner to indicate whether the vessel was either a Dundee ship or a stranger. At night, the Buddon lightkeepers fired a rocket and shone a blue light which was answered with a similar blue light from Broughty Castle. These signals were augmented in August 1839 when Charles Gray Esq. of Carse presented 'two beautiful carronade guns mounted on carriages of very complete construction.' One was mounted at Buddon and the other was placed on a platform within Broughty Castle.

These new arrangements were being finalised when, on the night of Saturday, 30 December 1837, the little Dundee brig *Thistle* went ashore on the Abertay Sands. The *Thistle* was under the command of Captain Alexander Keddie and his son James gave the following account of the wreck;

We entered the channel of the river about half-past ten o'clock on Saturday evening and soon after lost one of the south lights, owing either to the heavy mist that prevailed or to a ship's mast coming between us and it. Judging we were far enough north, we pursued our course up the river and soon after struck on the Elbow End. The Mate immediately went to the topmast to try and catch the lights and observed broken water on every side; we then made the signal for a boat by setting fire to a tar barrel. On sounding the pumps and finding six feet of water in the hold, we slipped the chain and endeavoured to wear the ship round. We had not proceeded far till we struck a second time on the Coal Bank, when we took to the boat which unhappily instantly swamped and threw the Mate and one of the men into the water.

The master, seeing that we should not live, advised that we should all take to the ship again. We continued three hours and a half after this in the rigging (five hours after we first struck) ere any assistance arrived. At last a fishing boat from North Ferry, with eight active young men, came to us and in a few minutes after three of the crew were rescued from the wreck and safely lodged in the boat. An attempt was then made to take the master and myself from the rigging; but my father was so much exhausted and benumbed with cold that he could do nothing for himself and I was almost equally unable. I therefore called for assistance from the boat when a brave and spirited young man, Alexander Gall, sprung to our aid, but unfortunately lost his hold and fell into the water, going right below the boat. On being recovered he made a second attempt and succeeded in reaching the place where we were; but, from the surging of the vessel and the dashing of the sea over us, both he and I lost hold of my father who fell into the water.

By this time, the lifeboat had arrived but I was so entangled in the rigging that it was some time before I got down to assist Gall who had got hold of my father again but was unable to keep him, having himself been severely bruised between the lifeboat and the wreck. I kept fast hold of my father for some time after Gall was taken into the lifeboat, but a heavy sea, with which I was by that time unable to contend, came and separated us in spite of every exertion I made, and we never saw him again. With considerable difficulty I was got into the lifeboat and carried to the light-house where I was most kindly treated. The three seamen were taken to the Ferry, and provided for in the most attentive manner there. Those of us who have been saved can never be grateful enough to kind-hearted and brave men who were the instruments of our deliverance.

Thistle had been in the news some months earlier when she picked up a cow that had fallen overboard from a steamer off the Dutch coast. Captain Keddie scrounged some hay from another ship and brought his seasick and distressed prize back to Dundee. The cow was sold to a travelling showman who painted black spots on its body and gave it a violet coloured belly and legs. Described as a 'Sea Cow', it was displayed at Newcastle surrounded by clams and oysters. Shrewd observers, however, noted that it preferred to eat hay and the hoax was exposed in the *Tyne Mercury*.

Peter Stark took the Buddon lifeboat to another ship ashore on the Abertay Sands on 14 January 1838. This time, the victim was the Prussian barque *Rhein* which had run aground after the leading lights were obscured by a snowstorm. *Rhein* sank quickly and the lifeboat took Captain Reick and his crew off after they had been four hours in the rigging.

Snow was the cause of another wreck on the Abertay Sands a month later on the night of Friday, 16 February. Captain John Laverick was bringing his schooner, the *Barjona* of Whitby, into Dundee with a cargo of 600 barrels of herring. Again, the lights were obscured by snow and Laverick lost the channel, grounding on the Abertay shortly before 4.00 a.m. The *Barjona* sank in under 30 minutes and, despite icy seas which swept three quarters of the way up the masts her crew took to the rigging. Peter Stark saw the wreck from Broughty Ferry at daybreak. With the help of a tow from Robert Knight's fishing yawl, he got the Buddon lifeboat alongside and took off Laverick, his four crew and two passengers.

At last, the lifeboat was beginning to attract some positive publicity. Following the *Barjona* service, the *Dundee Advertiser* commented, 'The greatest praise is due to Lt Stark for again distinguishing himself in so intrepid and successful a manner, and to Robert Knight who readily agreed to proceed to the wreck.' Half of the *Barjona's* cargo was saved and the lifeboat crew were each awarded 10/- (50p) by both the RNLI and the local society.

One of the last winter gales had just blown itself out three weeks later, on Saturday, 3 March, though a heavy sea was still running. That night, at about 6.30 p.m., the brig *Ranger* of Perth, bound from Newcastle for Dundee with coal, was becalmed in the channel and swept onto the Elbow End. She was soon heavily damaged as seas crashed her repeatedly onto the hard sand and, as she sank, her crew took refuge in the rigging. At first light, Peter Stark saw the mast of the *Ranger* sticking out of the water and the tiny figures of her five freezing crewmen clinging on for their lives. He immediately manned his own gig with eight hands and, accompanied by a fishing yawl, pulled down river to the Buddon lifeboat. The *Ranger's* crew of five were taken off safely despite the seas breaking over the wreck.

As ever, the River Tay Lifeboat and Humane Society was acutely short of money. Following the service to the *Ranger*, they were unable to pay the usual reward to the crew as there was simply nothing in the kitty. There were pointed suggestions in the press that, as the crew of the *Ranger* were all Perth men, the people of Perth could be more generous towards the lifeboat. The RNLI, however, stepped in, paying each of the crew 10/- (50p) and awarding Stark the rare honour of its gold medal.

Peter Stark had become something of a local hero. At a dinner in Wallace's Hotel in April 1838 he was presented with a salver and 100 guineas, and was made a Freeman of the City of Dundee in recognition of his having saved more than 60 lives*. Stark left Broughty Ferry at the beginning of September 1838 to take command of the Portpatrick to Donaghadee steam packet *Spitfire*. At 6.30 p.m. on Wednesday, 5 September, the Dundee and Hull Steam Packet

---

* With the lifeboat very much in the news at this time, a correspondent in the *Dundee Advertiser* suggested that the crew should be issued with an inflatable tube secured around the chest with leather straps. He felt that this, the precursor of the modern lifejacket, would make the crew more willing to go out in bad weather!

Company's *Forfarshire*, the same ship Stark had used in the attempted rescue of the crew of the *Mary* in 1836, steamed out of Hull docks on her regular run back to Dundee. Her starboard boiler sprang a leak in the early hours of the following morning. The leak was plugged, albeit with some difficulty, but reappeared that evening when *Forfarshire* was abeam of Berwick, and got progressively worse until boiler water was pouring into the bilges. This was pumped back into the boiler but, eventually, the pumps were unable to keep up and the ship lost all power.

The Dundee and Hull Steam Packet Company's steamer Forfarshire *was used by Coxswain Peter Stark in the attempted rescue of the crew of the* Mary *from the Abertay Sands on Boxing Day 1836. The* Forfarshire's *destruction on the reefs next to the Farne Islands in September 1838 cost the lives of more than 50 passengers and crew most of whom hailed from the Dundee area. The rescue of ten survivors by William Darling and his daughter Grace has passed into legend.*
(DUNDEE ART GALLERIES AND MUSEUMS)

A north-easterly gale blew up as the *Forfarshire's* engineers struggled with the leaking boiler and Captain John Humble decided to make sail and head for sheltered water in the lee of the Farne Islands. He appears to have confused the two lighthouses on the Farnes, the Longstone and the Inner Farne High, and sailed his ship straight onto the Big Hurcar Rock. *Forfarshire* struck at about 3.00 a.m. on Friday, 7 September, and broke up. The stern half sank quickly, taking with it Captain Humble and most of the passengers but 12 survivors managed to clamber onto the rock where they were seen by the Longstone lightkeeper, William Darling.

Darling and his daughter Grace rowed for about a mile in a small coble and took off the first group of five survivors, one of them a mother who had just watched her two children die of exposure. Two men took over at the oars and, after landing Grace and the other survivors, William Darling and his two oarsmen returned to the wreck to collect the five who remained. Grace Darling's place as the frail heroine at the centre of a rather over-romanticised Victorian legend was assured when she died of tuberculosis four years later.

Chapter Three

THAT CELEBRATED, EXPERIENCED AND THOROUGHLY EFFICIENT CORPORATION

On Saturday, 6 October 1838, a month after the loss of the *Forfarshire*, Dundee newspapers carried intimations of the forthcoming auction of her remains, some of which were still lying on the Hurcar. That afternoon, amid scenes of wild excitement, the Dundee and Arbroath Railway opened for business. The inaugural train of ten carriages left the Roodyards terminus in Dundee at midday for the 36 minute journey to Arbroath. In an open carriage immediately behind the smoke-belching engine stood a rather grimy brass band playing, apparently incessantly, *See The Conquering Hero Comes.*

Despite the opening of the new railway, Dundee's communications with the outside world had changed little since the Middle Ages. Travellers to Glasgow in 1838 still had to endure an eleven and three quarter hour journey by coach and sedan chairs were still common on Dundee streets. News of the death of King William IV, and the accession of Queen Victoria, in June 1837 took almost two days to reach the city.

The Victorian era was to see Dundee's population almost double from barely 58,000 to over 100,000 in just 50 years. Business at Dundee Harbour multiplied as textile manufacture expanded rapidly and landward communications improved. Shipping using the Tay grew in both numbers and size as the city's trade took on a truly worldwide character. The first bales of jute arrived at the Earl Grey Dock aboard the barque *Selma* in April 1840.

By no means all of the ships wrecked on the coastlines of Angus and Fife were destined for the River Tay. Many were bound for distant ports only to be blown, at the mercy of a gale, into St Andrews Bay. One such was the 400 ton brig *Petrel*, a new and well-found vessel bound for Grangemouth from North America with a cargo of timber. Captain David Parry reached what he thought was the entrance to the River Forth in heavy snow late on Friday, 29 November 1839. Suddenly, through a break in the blizzard, his men sighted the Buddon Ness lights. In weather said to be as, 'thick as a hedge,' Parry desperately tried to fight his way clear of the bay. Surf breaking on the Fife shore loomed out of the darkness and he tried to anchor, but it was too late and the *Petrel* crashed ashore at Buddo Rock, west of Boarhills.

The sole survivor from the *Petrel*, her Second Mate, Henry Thoms, was thrown ashore along with some floating wreckage. Despite a broken leg, he crawled more that 300 yards up the beach towards Burnside Farmhouse and was found by tenant farmer Mr Adamson who sent for the coastguard from St Andrews. The wreck, meanwhile, had been discovered by St Andrews fishermen Jack Wilson and Willie Chisholm. The *Petrel's* eight dead crewmen and one passenger, a Mrs Westgarth, were buried in the little churchyard at Boarhills.

A coastguard from St Andrews was still standing guard over the cargo of the *Petrel* when another ship was seen standing in to the bay on the morning of Friday, 19 December. The *Isabella and Ann* of Aberdeen was bound for Dundee with a cargo of coal. In heavy seas, she was swept past the entrance to the Tay and into the shoals behind the Abertay Sands. Henry Cox launched the *Volunteer Lifeboat* from the West Sands and had her rowed round to St Andrews Harbour. There, he waited to see if the wind would change to a more westerly direction with the start of the ebb tide, thus allowing the ship to sail herself out of trouble. By 3.00 p.m. it was clear that this would not happen.

After rowing for two hours, the lifeboatmen reached the *Isabella and Ann* just as she was about to strike the bottom. As they got alongside, Henry Cox and bowman Davie Henderson were washed overboard but were quickly hauled back aboard. A narrow channel, known as 'The Pool' and navigable at certain states of tide, lies between the Abertay Sands and Tentsmuir Point. With great skill, Cox and his men piloted the *Isabella and Ann* through this channel into the Tay in pitch darkness and brought her safely to anchor off Tayport. The *Volunteer Lifeboat* was taken back to St Andrews on her carriage. Her crew, however, walked home. Henry Cox was awarded the RNLI's silver medal.

Another coal ship brought three RNLI silver medals to St Andrews in October 1841 when the Guardbridge-bound sloop *Thomas and George* was wrecked on the Burnstools off the harbour entrance. Jack Wilson and two coastguards accompanied Henry Cox to the wreck in a fishing boat and rescued the crew of five. The wreck was carried up onto the the East Sands and was a ready source of free coal for the local needy during that winter.

Salvage of a different kind was at hand just over a week later, on the evening of Friday, 29 October 1841, after Captain Meikle tried to bring the Bo'ness registered brig *Vestal* into the Tay without a pilot. He first struck the Elbow End then drifted across the river to ground on the Gaa Sands. News that the *Vestal* was laden with wine from Oporto soon reached Broughty Ferry and Tayport and local fishermen wasted no time in getting aboard to help themselves. It was said that they rapidly became 'quite uproarious.'

With all the righteous indignation it could muster, the *Dundee Advertiser* growled;

> The conduct of the fishermen who were assisting in saving that wreck was very bad, the desire for drink having got completely the better of them. Even on Sunday, many, both men and women, in Broughty and Ferry-Port-on-Craig were intoxicated. The Revenue Officers at first attempted to keep order but in the end we understand that they too gave way to the allurement of the wine. Such conduct is highly reprehensible and will, we trust, be investigated.

Henry Cox had left St Andrews when, in the winter of 1845, the Great Yarmouth steamer *Po* found herself in trouble off the entrance to the River Eden. The *Volunteer Lifeboat* was launched under her new coxswain, Jack Wilson, and the chief boatman of the coastguard, John Gregory. They got alongside the *Po* at about 3.00 p.m. and convinced her captain that his ship was in imminent danger of striking bottom. The crew of the *Po* were brought ashore at about 6.00 p.m. and all concerned repaired to the Bell Rock Tavern to celebrate.

In their hasty departure from their ship, the *Po*'s crew had inadvertently left their distress signal flying which meant that she was legally abandoned and anyone could have salvage of her, even if she had not gone ashore. Andrew Brown and Willie Chisholm, both experienced pilots and fishermen, saw their chance. Along with Willie Chisholm's brother Jack and four lads they found courting by the Old Abbey Wall, they slipped quietly out of the harbour in Andrew Brown's fishing boat. As they did so, they passed close to the Bell Rock Tavern from where they could hear the lifeboatmen and the crew of the *Po* loudly enjoying themselves.

Somebody went into the inn a few minutes later and announced, 'There's a yawl awa' aff tae yer ship, Captain.' The *Po*'s crew all jumped up, according to one observer, 'as if an explosion of dynamite had taken place in the cellar below.' The captain ran out of the door, cursing as only a seafarer can, and yelling for another boat to be got ready to sail. He declared that if he catched the d——d b——-s on board his ship, he would treat them as pirates and throw them into the sea. The *Po* was actually touching bottom when Brown and his crew boarded her but they managed to make sail and catch the first of the flood tide for the Tay. The furious captain was forced to look on impotently as his ship was got under way and, still vowing vengeance, he settled the salvage claim in Dundee the following day.

It is said that, soon after the *Po* incident, an Irish sloop got into trouble near the mouth of the Eden and the *Volunteer Lifeboat* was launched to her aid. News travels surprisingly fast in the maritime community and, when they pulled alongside, the lifeboatmen were treated to a torrent of colourful celtic abuse.

Andrew 'Boy' Brown's enterprise did him no harm at all as he was later made coxswain of the *Volunteer Lifeboat*. Willie Chisholm subsequently took over as coxswain when Brown emigrated to Australia, but not before one rather embarrassing incident in December 1848. The brand new Prussian barque *Johann Freidrich* was coming into Dundee to have her hull copper sheathed before proceeding to Buenos Aires. Captain Bradhering had secured Chisholm's services as pilot and the *Johann Freidrich* was following another vessel up the channel when it disappeared in a heavy shower of snow. The snow disorientated Chisholm and he ran the

Johann Freidrich straight on to the the Abertay Sands at the back of no. 4 buoy.

For some reason, the Prussians completely failed to see the funny side of this and expressed a strongly-worded desire to throw him over the side. The hapless Chisholm had to take refuge in the rigging until Buddon Ness lifeboat appeared in tow of the steamer *Captain Craig* and took all 14 off the *Johann Freidrich*. Dundee Harbourmaster Captain John Jack said that Bradhering would have been far safer without a pilot. The *Johann Freidrich* was refloated before the end of the month and towed up to Dundee by an inbound steam packet. Bought by Alexander Stephen & Co, the Dundee shipbuilders, she was refitted, renamed *Stephano,* and operated for many years thereafter in the China Sea.

The first five Tay Pilots had been licensed in January 1839 as river traffic began to grow with industrialisation. Within ten years the pilotage business had become fiercely competitive and boatloads of fishermen were roaming around off the Tay in search of inbound shipping. By 1849 there were 49 licensed pilots mainly Galls, Andersons, Ferriers, Websters, Norries and Kidds fom Broughty Ferry along with Cargills and Swankies from Arbroath. This was a clearly ludicrous situation as nobody could hope to make a decent living. The position was resolved in 1850 when the licences of all but 12 pilots and two supernumaries were revoked. Captain John Spink was appointed pilotmaster and the Fraternity of Masters and Seamen bought the first, purpose-built pilot cutter, the *Happy Return.*

Considerable attention was also paid to the improvement of lighting and buoyage. The lights at Buddon Ness were redesigned and a black stripe was painted on the Buddon High light to make it more visible against snow. Arguments had been raging for years over the advisability of stationing a lightship to mark the Elbow End. A series of formal hearings on the subject lasted for six months from January 1847. Evidence was taken from a wide range of people including Broughty Ferry fishermen, shipmasters and shipowners. The balance of opinion was firmly against a lightship. Some felt that, as the channel was so narrow, a lightship might itself prove a hazard to navigation. Others, mainly shipowners, had at least one eye on the increased harbour dues that the building and maintenance of a lightship would incur.

The modernisation of both the pilotage service and the buoyage was matched by the renovation of the management of the River Tay Lifeboat and Humane Society which, on 20 June 1850, was reconstituted as a joint committee of the Fraternity of Masters and Seamen and the Harbour Trustees. Patrick Just retired as secretary and was succeeded by James McEwen. Shore Dues Collector Simon Robertson continued as treasurer and Captain James Neish was elected chairman.

At about this time, in addition to the boat already moored off Buddon Ness, new lifeboats were stationed, one on a mooring off Ferryport-on-Craig, as Tayport was then known, and one at Magdalen Green. The Tayport lifeboat was intended, in part, to provide safety cover for the steam ferries operating between the new railheads at Tayport and Broughty Ferry. One of the early ferries, the *Comet,* had sunk after ramming Tayport Harbour breakwater on a dark night in December 1848, though her passengers managed to scramble ashore. From March 1851, the *Robert Napier* and the *Carrier* took rail wagons back and forth across the river, thus avoiding the long detour via Perth*.

Magdalen Green lifeboat operated from a set of launching rails at Buckingham Point, now the landfall for the Tay Bridge, and was a means of rescue for bathers and boating parties at this popular Victorian leisure spot. Sadly, no record of services rendered by the Magdalen Green lifeboat has survived. It is possible, however, that she was manned by members of the Royal Naval Coast Volunteers, predecessors of the modern Royal Naval Reserve, who trained at Buckingham Point prior to the arrival of their first drill ship, HMS *Brilliant,* in 1862.

---

* Relations between the Lifeboat and Humane Society and the Edinburgh, Perth and Dundee Railway Co. were rather less than cordial. The railway company had purchased Broughty Castle for use as a store and summarily ordered the society to remove all its rockets and signalling apparatus, including the presentation carronades.

The early 1850s also saw a much-needed improvement in the organisation of the RNLI. The institution had been in the doldrums throughout the previous decade, particularly since the death of its founder, Sir William Hillary, in 1847. It took the loss of 20 lifeboatmen with the South Shields lifeboat *Providence* in December 1849 to stir the nation's conscience. A new dynamism was injected when Rear Admiral the Duke of Northumberland took up the long-vacant post of President, Richard Lewis was appointed Secretary and Commander J.R. Ward RN became the Institution's Inspector of Lifeboats. *The Lifeboat* journal was first published in March 1852, a fixed scale of remuneration for coxswains and crews was established and a programme of regular inspections of RNLI lifeboat stations was begun.

Both the St Andrews and River Tay lifeboat societies remained independent of the RNLI throughout the 1850s and all four lifeboats continued to provide life-saving services. Buddon lifeboat saved five when the schooner *Margaret* was wrecked on the Abertay Sands on Wednesday, 8 December 1852. On 28 October the following year, the Buddon boat saved the six crew of the schooner *Elizabeth*, inbound for Dundee with timber, which was wrecked on the Elbow End. Just over a month later, the Tayport lifeboat went down river in a strong south-westerly gale to rescue the nine crew of the *Vesta*, a brig inbound with flax from Cronstadt.

Dundee's rapid industrial expansion led to a huge growth in the demand for timber. The North Shields brig *Gleaner* entered the Tay on the morning of Sunday, 23 December 1855 with a cargo of Canadian timber. A stiff southerly breeze was accompanied by heavy snow showers and an uncomfortable sea. As happened to so many masters before him, Captain John Wilson found that a snow shower obscured the Buddon lights at just the wrong moment and he was completely blind. He ran onto the banks and his crew of 10 were rescued by Buddon lifeboat four hours later, just as their ship began to break up under them.

Buddon lifeboat was manned by Westhaven men when the *Diana* lost her way and attempted unsuccessfully to cross the Gaa Bank while inbound for Dundee from Hamburg on the evening of 15 April 1856. Captain Ostmann and his crew of four were landed at Buddon at 10.00 p.m. The wreck of their ship was carried over the Gaa on the flood tide and grounded on the south shore of the river from where it was later salvaged by fishermen.

An error, often made by mariners unfamiliar with the east coast of Scotland, was to mistake Fife Ness at the south end of St Andrews Bay for St Abbs Head at the southern entrance to the River Forth. The master of the barley-laden *Dagmar* made precisely this blunder on 31 March 1857 and sailed straight onto the Abertay Sands. He and his crew of five were picked up from the wreck by Buddon lifeboat.

The jute-laden schooner *Peace* was inbound for Dundee on 23 April 1859 and was being followed into the river by another schooner, the *Heernveen* of Memel, also bound for Dundee but with a cargo of flax. A south-easterly gale was blowing and visibility was bad when both ships missed the channel and found themselves stranded on the south side of the Abertay Sands.

Both the Tayport and Buddon Ness lifeboats were manned and, as Harbourmaster John Jack wrote;

Captain Adamson with his steamer got the South Ferry [Tayport] lifeboat in tow and proceeded down river to the stranded vessels, and also went to the Sea Lights and rendered some assistance to the other boat and I am of the opinion it was from [his] assistance that the lifeboats were put in a position to render any assistance and much praise is due to Captain Adamson and the crews of both lifeboats for their conduct in this matter.

Jack states that, 'with great exertion,' one lifeboat was pulled through the breakers to one of the stranded schooners only to be told that the crew did not wish to leave. In the event, both schooners were driven over the bank as the tide rose and got into deeper water little damaged.

The 1850s were relatively quiet years for the St Andrews *Volunteer Lifeboat*. One incident did, however, cause much excitement. The foundation stone of what is now the R&A clubhouse was laid with full masonic ceremonial on Wednesday, 13 July 1853. It was hoped that the fine weather that had blessed the ceremony would continue for the games planned for the following day. One of the events was to be a rowing race and, that evening, the crews of three boats practised by pulling round a brig anchored off the town. Many of the oarsmen commented on the freshening easterly breeze.

The wind increased to a full easterly gale overnight and a torrential rainstorm began around mid-morning. Despite the storm, a few events were contested before the games were abandoned about 3.00 p.m.. With tongue firmly in cheek, the *Fifeshire Journal* reported that;

> On dispersion of the meeting the people flocked into the town, some traversing the streets, parties grouping into doors and entries, others visiting accessible lions. But we should imagine that the dispensation was especially in favour of the public houses which must have been troubled, or rather favoured, with over-population. The City Hall was open; many went in and found intellectual entertainment in the form of a homily on the excellencies of total abstinence. But for the convenience of the shelter, we suspect the audience would have found another resort. The grand spectacle of the day, however, was yet to come, a scene never premeditated in the day's programme, but surpassing all others in novelties and spirit-stirring effect.

The brig round which the oarsmen had practised the night before, the *Cybele* of Dundee, had arrived off St Andrews about a week earlier with timber from New Brunswick. Owing to the prevailing neap tides there was insufficient depth of water for her to enter the harbour and she had anchored off, discharging part of her cargo by rafting it ashore. There had been considerable speculation about her ability to ride out the storm and, just as the games were abandoned at 3.00 p.m., the first of her two anchor cables parted. The other cable broke about an hour later leaving the brig adrift and rushing headlong towards a lee shore. Her crew managed to hoist sufficient sail to carry her past the Burnstools and she careered onto the Hornal Dub, about 400 yards off the East Sands.

A first attempt at rescue by seven fishermen, though daring and courageous, came perilously close to disaster as their yawl was almost swamped several times and had to return to harbour. Meanwhile, the *Volunteer Lifeboat* was being brought across town from her boatshed next to the Swilcan Burn. It was the work of just a few minutes to launch her from the East Sands, row out to the *Cybele* and take her crew aboard. On hearing the cry, 'Ship Ashore!' thousands of holidaymakers had gathered at every vantage point from the sands to the pierhead. They gave a rousing cheer as the lifeboat pulled into the harbour.

In the summer of 1859, as the first transatlantic telegraph cable came into operation and Charles Darwin's *Origin of the Species* neared publication, the RNLI began to increase its representation in Scotland. They offered new lifeboats, paid coxswains, 'liberal' remuneration to lifeboat crews* and many new lifeboat stations were established as a result. St Andrews lifeboat station was one of a number of hitherto private stations that expressed an interest in joining the institution. Next to advertisements for lost pets, cattle feed and painless tooth extraction, the classified section of *Fifeshire Journal* for Thursday, 29 December 1859 contains the following notice;

APPEAL

THE ROYAL NATIONAL LIFEBOAT INSTITUTION having had a first-class lifeboat and gear placed at their disposal by an English gentleman resident in London, and knowing the inefficiency of the present lifeboat stationed at St Andrews from the report of their Inspector, Commander Ward R.N.; and taking into account the dangerous nature of St Andrews Bay, and its proximity to the much frequented shipping waters of the Forth and Tay, have voluntarily offered to station the boat above referred to at St Andrews.

---

* Remuneration has never been exactly liberal. In 1996, a volunteer crewman receives just £7 for a service launch, or 'shout', with a supplement of £2 per hour after the first hour - and even that is taxable. Money has never been an inducement for lifeboat crews. Lifeboat crews also receive £3 for every exercise launch. The Broughty Ferry crew pool this money towards an annual dinner dance attended by all crew, former crew and committee members.

The appeal went on to state that the old *Volunteer Lifeboat* had saved 96 lives since 1824 and that a sum of £250 had to be raised to pay for the construction of a boatshed and a carriage for the new boat. There was clearly a ready response as, at 3.00 p.m. on 31 January 1860, a large crowd assembled to watch the new St Andrews lifeboat *Annie* paraded through the streets of the town.

Brought north to Dundee by steamer, the *Annie* had been taken across to Newport that morning by ferry. The St Andrews magistrates were not about to miss this golden opportunity to associate themselves with such a worthy cause and had arranged for the lifeboat to be drawn by teams of horses through Tayport, Leuchars and Guardbridge to St Andrews. Had wiser heads prevailed, she would have been brought round from Dundee by sea. As it was, what had been intended as a triumphal progress rapidly degenerated into an embarrassing fiasco.

Mounted on her carriage, the boat was being unloaded at Newport Pier when a wheel slipped off the ramp to land on the stonework with a crash that broke the axle. This was repaired and, decked out with bunting and flags, the boat set out for St Andrews. She was already far too late for the planned parade when, at 5.00 p.m., the procession arrived at Guardbridge. The magistrates had ignored warnings about the narrowness of Bishop Wardlaw's bridge over the River Eden and, inevitably, the procession came to a shuddering halt as the wheels of the carriage jammed solid between the parapets. 'Much noise and confusion,' ensued as over an hour was wasted in fruitless attempts at getting across. The *Annie* was finally launched into the Eden and rowed round to St Andrews, arriving, 'just in time for a glass of grog,' at 11.00 p.m.

The Home Hole at St Andrews in 1840. At right, next to the famous Swilcan Bridge, is the boatshed built for the Volunteer Lifeboat *in 1824. In 1864, this boatshed was dismantled and rebuilt five miles away at Boarhills where it housed the old* Volunteer Lifeboat *for another 17 years. It was enlarged in 1881 to house the new Boarhills lifeboat* John and James Mills *and is now a cattleshed.*
(ST ANDREWS UNIVERSITY)

A large crowd assembled at the new boatshed on the East Bents when the *Annie* was launched for her first trial on Saturday, 10 March 1860. She had been built to a standard RNLI design drawn up by the assistant master shipwright at Woolwich Naval Dockyard, James Peake. Fully self-righting, she was 32 feet long with a beam of eight feet and was propelled either by sail or ten oarsmen. Fisherman James Morgan was appointed first coxswain and Willie Chisholm was made second coxswain. The *Annie's* first service was to stand by five local fishing yawls caught in a gale on 3 October 1860.

The River Tay Lifeboat and Humane Society were markedly less willing to lose their independence to the RNLI and, in 1859, they had a new lifeboat built at Calman and Martin's Dundee shipyard. The society based their new boat on the standard Peake design but, in several significant areas, felt that they knew more about the design of lifeboats than the RNLI. In the Peake-designed boat, large, bulbous air-cases fore and aft provided the buoyancy that helped give the boat her self-righting capability. These were greatly reduced in size in the River Tay lifeboat as the society felt that this would make the boat more streamlined and easier to row into the wind.

The new boat was launched for the first time into King William IV Dock at the end of October 1859. She was certainly faster and had better self-emptying capabilities than the old 1830 boat. In one crucial respect, however, she was a total failure. Due in part to the reduction in the size of the air-cases, she resolutely refused to right herself when capsized in the calm waters of the dock. Indeed, she would only turn upright with the assistance of a crane.

Lifeboats designed on the self-righting principle have always been 'lively' boats and give the impression of greater instability than the heavier, non-self-righting boats. A supposedly self-righting boat, that was manifestly incapable of doing so, was not about to endear herself to those expected to man her. Despite her well-known shortcomings, the society insisted on stationing the new boat at Buddon Ness, an odd decision as this placed her where she would have to operate in the fiercest sea conditions.

The Calman and Martin boat was used only twice. On the first occasion, in relatively calm conditions in July 1861, she took off the crew of the Peterhead schooner *Recruit* which had stranded on the Abertay Sands. Her second and final service took place on the clear, frosty evening of Monday, 11 November 1861. The Norwegian brigantine *Marionne* had passed the fairway buoy at 4.00 p.m., inbound for Dundee from Frederickstadt with a cargo of timber. The pilot cutter had been trapped in the Tay by bad weather so Captain Neilsen attempted to enter on his own but ran his ship ashore on the Abertay Sands. The action of the wind, sea and tide combined to push the *Marionne* along the sandbank until she came to a halt directly opposite the Buddon Ness lifeboat station.

George Donaldson and Charles Findlay sailed down to Buddon Ness in their fishing boats only to find the Calman and Martin lifeboat half full of water that should have automatically drained through the relieving valves. They took the lifeboat in tow, bailing her out as they crossed the river to the *Marionne,* and reached the scene of the wreck at about 8.00 p.m..

Moonlight shone brightly over a steely blue sea and breakers rolled across the banks to burst into sheets of silver spray as they crashed against the stranded brigantine. Coxswain David Knight and his crew took one look at the sea conditions on the banks, another look at their water-logged, unseaworthy charge and abandoned any attempt at rescue as suicidal. Quite simply, the crew of the *Marionne* were, for the present, much safer where they were. The lifeboat was rowed up to Broughty Ferry and David Knight waited until midnight by which time the tide had gone out, providing a partial lee behind the banks. The eight crew of the *Marionne* were taken off in calmer conditions at 1.00 a.m. and landed at Buddon Ness.

Press reaction to this debacle was immediate and hostile. As the lifeboat crew waited at Broughty Ferry for better conditions on the banks, and with the fate of the *Marionne's* crew still uncertain, the *Dundee Advertiser* rushed into print with a scathing editorial which asked;

Why have we not a model boat, capable of righting herself and emptying herself? Why have we no trained crew familiar with lifeboat duty? And why have we no fixed and certain liberal rate of reward to encourage the lifeboatmen to risk their lives, and to act so as to be able to tell us something better than the melancholy story which we are grieved to have to submit to our readers this morning? It may be time to consider seriously whether Dundee should not get a boat from the Royal National Lifeboat Institution and place this boat and her crew under the management of that celebrated, experienced and thoroughly efficient corporation.

To add insult to already grievous injury, it was discovered that the Lifeboat and Humane Society were, as usual, 'without a farthing.' On behalf of the society, Secretary James McEwen at first tried to refute the allegations of incompetence but the writing was clearly on the wall. On Tuesday, 19 November, McEwen wrote to the RNLI referring to the *Marionne* incident, 'when the lifeboats were found to be very inefficient,' and stated that the River Tay Lifeboat and Humane Society had agreed to ask the RNLI to assume the management of their boats.

The RNLI management committee met on 5 December and agreed to take over and renovate the establishments at both Dundee and Dublin.

Construction of a new boatshed at the bottom of Fort Street in Broughty Ferry was begun almost immediately and, on 5 March 1862, indefatigable fund-raiser Mrs Mary Hartley of Bideford in Devon agreed to the lifeboat that would bear her name being stationed there. The *Mary Hartley* was similar to the *Annie* stationed at St Andrews two years earlier. Built by Forrestt of Limehouse at a cost of £190, she left London on 18 March aboard the D.P.&L. steamer *London*. Captain Thomas Ewing could have been forgiven for taking a certain proprietorial interest in his very special deck cargo; under the new RNLI regime, he had been appointed boats superintendent for the River Tay lifeboats.

The first trial of the new lifeboat took place four days later on Saturday, 22 March. Members of the new Dundee branch committee and, 'a select party of gentlemen of great nautical experience,' were conveyed down river to Buddon Ness in the steam tug *Samson*. With wry good humour, the reporter assigned to the event by the *Dundee Advertiser* wrote that,

> The weather, though dull and cold in the early part of the day, broke up beautifully about two o'clock, and a stiff breeze from the north-east, though occasioning most unpleasant sensations in the interior economy of landsmen, rendered the afternoon a most admirable one for practising the lifeboats.

The *Mary Hartley* and the original 1830 Robson lifeboat were waiting when the *Samson* arrived at Buddon Ness. The crews of both boats were brought aboard the steamer and treated to a rousing address by Major George Alison, a member of the committee. They were then served with substantial supplies of bread and beef and a glass of grog before being ordered to board their respective boats. The trials took place in heavy surf on the Abertay and Gaa Sands.

The *Advertiser*'s man recorded that, towards the end of the trial,

> The *Mary Hartley* made for the Gaa Sands between Nos. 3 and 4 (red) buoys, and hardly had she passed them when she was caught amidships by a curling roller and, poised for an instant on its crest, was whirled round end-on and carried with the velocity of an arrow for five or six hundred yards into comparatively smooth water. The sudden stroke of the wave caused two of the oars to snap, a number of the strong galvanised rowlocks were bent and the hat of one of the gallant volunteers was blown off.

In stark contrast to its editorial of four months earlier, the Advertiser enthused about the new boat,

> ...her thorough adaptability to the duties she may be called on to perform, her speed, her buoyancy, her model, and her self-emptying and self-righting qualities are as near perfection as may be and will place Dundee in a position of efficiency as never before in the saving of lives from shipwreck.

On completion of the trials, the old Robson lifeboat was returned to her station at Buddon Ness. Broughty Ferry fisherman George Anderson was appointed her coxswain. The *Mary Hartley* was towed up to the new station at Broughty Ferry, hauled out on her specially designed carriage and placed in the care of Coxswain John Knight. The lifeboat that had been moored off Tayport had seen very little use and the station was abandoned. The failed Calman and Martin boat was towed quietly away to Dundee to await the next steamer for London.

Meanwhile, the gentlemen aboard the *Samson* were treated to, 'an excellent cold collation served by Mr Macnaughton of the Royal Hotel.' Numerous toasts rounded off what could only have been a thoroughly jolly afternoon.

Chapter Four

FEARS TOO CRUELLY CONFIRMED

The first service by the River Tay lifeboats under the new RNLI regime was carried out a month prior to the arrival of the *Mary Hartley*. The little 98 ton Newburgh registered schooner *Elizabeth and Hannah* missed the channel while inbound with a cargo of fertiliser at 2.00 p.m. on a foggy Friday, 21 February 1862. Her predicament, stranded amid the surf on the Gaa Sands, was seen by Captain William Speedy of the steam packet *Hamburgh* and he immediately made for Buddon. There he found fishermen already manning the old lifeboat which he towed back down river and as close to the wreck as he dared.

Coxswain Tom Webster had great difficulty in getting the lifeboat alongside the stranded schooner. Finally, contact was made by floating a line down to her and hauling the lifeboat alongside. Six survivors, one of whom missed his footing and had to be pulled from the sea, were landed at Broughty Ferry at 8.00 p.m. The schooner was refloated five months later by fishermen who were awarded £600 for her salvage.

Scotland was well and truly in the grip of railway mania in 1862 and new lines, many of dubious viability, were threading out across the country. On Saturday, 1 November, the schooner *James Dowell* arrived off the Tay from Newcastle with a cargo of railway chairs and sleepers, and a serious leak. Captain Redhead and his crew abandoned her in the Tay channel and, on landing at Buddon Ness, fired signal rockets to summon the lifeboat crew. Seven fishing yawls were quickly on the scene and the Buddon lifeboat spent the night lashed alongside the schooner until a steam tug arrived the following morning.

Difficulties with the Tay pilotage service had persisted despite the improvements made in 1850. The pilot cutter was nowhere to be seen on the morning of 3 December 1862 when the inbound schooners *Osprey* of Fraserburgh and *Guttenberg* of Lubeck arrived off the river on the tail end of a gale. The flooding tide and strong easterly wind left Captain William Noble of the *Osprey* little option but to attempt the channel without a pilot. Captain Reimers of the *Guttenberg,* clearly under the impression that Noble knew where he was going, decided to follow. *Osprey* got safely past no. 2 buoy but was pushed west by the incoming tide and struck hard on the Elbow End. Captain Reimers in the *Guttenberg* was so close astern that he rammed *Osprey*'s stern and pushed her over the bank into deeper water where she promptly sank. Having sealed the *Osprey*'s fate, Reimers then ran aground himself.

As the tide rose, the *Guttenberg* was washed over the bank, past the wreck of the *Osprey* and into deep water. The *Osprey*'s crew were clinging for dear life to the rigging of their sunken ship and were not in the least amused by Reimer's shouted refusal to lend them the *Guttenberg*'s rowing boat. The pilot cutter was attempting to come down river against the tide and, at 10.00 a.m., three pilots rowed ashore at Buddon Ness to fire the signal gun.

Buddon Ness lifeboat was thought to be better placed than the *Mary Hartley,* so Coxswain George Anderson and 16 crewmen walked the six miles and unmoored at midday. The six crew of the *Osprey* were picked up after spending four hours in the rigging. The leaking *Guttenberg,* meanwhile, had been beached off Monifieth. St Andrews lifeboat was also launched that afternoon when a Swedish ship was seen in trouble off the town. The *Annie*'s crew were somewhat bemused when the Swedish captain asked if he was off Sunderland.

The *Mary Hartley*'s first service took place at 9.30 a.m. on Sunday, 4 January 1863 when she picked up the crew of the ketch *Neuha* that had gone ashore on the Abertay Sands. The *Neuha*'s crew had got away in their small boat but, as it was blowing hard from the east, this too was in imminent danger of sinking.

Buddon Ness lifeboat undertook the next service at daybreak on Saturday, 10 October 1863 after the Palermo registered schooner *Giulia* of Captain Fardelli, inbound with flax from Cronstadt, was seen anchored in shoal water off Westhaven. Having been used to pass a hawser to the *Giulia* from the tug *Samson,* the lifeboat was then secured astern of the *Giulia* for the tow into the river. While crossing The Bar, however, she was swamped by a large wave and disappeared.

Samson towed the *Giulia* up to anchor off Broughty Ferry. The lifeboat crew then set off to search for their wayward charge which they found lying on the beach a little west of Carnoustie. After saving something of the order of 90 lives in 33 years, this was to be the last service for the original 1830 lifeboat. She was old, leaky and worn out and sank at her mooring during a gale on 9 December 1863. As there were numerous steamers available to tow the *Mary Hartley* down river from Broughty Ferry, it was felt that Buddon Ness station could close, at least for a trial period.

Fearful storms raged across Britain for three days from Friday, 21 October 1864 and a number of vessels were damaged, driven ashore or sunk in the Firths of Forth and Clyde. The gale was at its height over the east coast by the Sunday morning. St Andrews Bay was a mass of boiling seas and huge waves were being hurled against the rocky shore east of the town. A large brig was seen crossing the bay from the north at midday and it was obvious to the crowd on the Kirkhill that she was in great danger. At 1.20 p.m., she was flung onto the Outer Luckies, a 300 yard long reef off Boarhills.

The *Annie*'s crew had assembled as soon as the danger to the brig was seen, but attempting a launch from the East Sands and rowing into the storm for almost five miles to the wreck was clearly out of the question. Some suggested taking the lifeboat to Boarhills where there was a small creek used by local fishermen. Coxswain Alex Mackrell argued that, as there would be little more than a foot of clearance beyond the ends of the oars on either side, the *Annie* would be dashed to pieces against the rocks. John Purvis, Secretary of the St Andrews lifeboat, agreed

Inward bound for the Fairway. A brig crossing St Andrews Bay.
(SUSAN HUGHAN)

and sent a rider to collect the Manby Rocket Apparatus from the coastguard station at Crail*.

The brig had struck at low water but between her crew and dry land lay a number of deep water channels rendered impassable by the storm. One brave man was seen to jump in a desperate bid for the shore but was immediately dashed against the rocks and disappeared. His body was found some days later, the legs and arms broken and the head missing. The rest of the brig's crew took to the rigging as their ship began to break up underneath them, their wretched cries for help clearly audible to those on the shore.

It was clear that the only possible means of rescue would be the rocket apparatus on its way from Crail. This finally arrived shortly after 4.00 p.m. but it was discovered that only five rockets were available as the other 20 had been fired off by coastguards at a recent exercise and not replaced. The five rockets were duly fired towards the wreck but all failed to reach her. In the gathering darkness at 5.30 p.m., as the tide rose, the brig heeled over and broke up, pitching the last of her unfortunate crew to their deaths. From the wreckage, she was identified as the *Napoleon* of Udevalla in Norway, three days out of Sunderland. The bodies of her crew lie in the graveyard at Boarhills Church.

The Fife press largely agreed with John Purvis and Coxswain Mackrell that to have attempted a launch from Boarhills would have been an act of considerable folly. From the other side of the Tay, however, the *Dundee Advertiser* fired off a vitriolic attack on the St Andrews Lifeboat Committee. The *Advertiser* even suggested that the people of St Andrews and Boarhills were callous and unfeeling, and that the *Annie,* 'was of no earthly use except as a holiday spectacle.' In an atmosphere of mounting hysteria, some said that the lifeboat crew were too old and unfit, others suggested that the lifeboat committee were overly concerned with the condition of the *Annie's* paintwork. As is usual in such cases, those loudest in their criticism enjoyed all the benefits afforded by hindsight.

Moving a lifeboat around on land in the 1860s was no easy matter. Four tons of lifeboat mounted on a heavy carriage had to be hauled over primitive roads by teams of at least four horses. When, amid the mounting confusion at Boarhills, the order was finally sent to bring the lifeboat, hauling the *Annie* the five miles from St Andrews by road took well over an hour. She arrived at 5.30 p.m., just as the *Napoleon* broke up.

The Crail coastguards were certainly remiss in not having replenished their stock of rockets. Had they done so, it is likely that a line could have been got aboard the wreck and most of her crew saved. It is also possible to argue that the lifeboat should have been sent to Boarhills by road immediately the *Napoleon* was seen to strike. Both the Board of Trade and the RNLI, however, were clear in their view that to attempt a launch from Boarhills in the prevailing conditions would have been suicidal.

St Andrews lifeboat was the butt of further press attacks only a month later after the Prussian barque *Sidonia* was seen in difficulties in the bay at midday on Thursday 24 November. Bound for Norway with a cargo of coal from the Tyne, she had been within sight of the Norwegian coast when an easterly gale blew up and forced her all the way back across the North Sea into St Andrews Bay.

As she battled against the storm, a fierce and bitter argument took place among the onlookers gathered on the Kirkhill. It was abundantly clear to most of those present that the listing *Sidonia* was flying a distress signal. Inexplicably, Coxswain Mackrell preferred to believe that she was merely flying the signal requesting a pilot and refused to launch the lifeboat. Second Coxswain Willie Chisholm entertained no such doubts and wished to launch right away, but he was overruled and the *Sidonia* was left to her own devices. That night, when the wind veered to the south-east, she managed to get clear of St Andrews Bay only to be wrecked near Banff some hours later. One of her crew, a 13 year old boy, was drowned during the subsequent rescue.

---

* Captain George Manby, a founder member of the RNLI, first adapted a mortar to fire rocket lines across stranded vessels at Great Yarmouth in 1829. A heavier line was then passed on which men could be brought ashore in a breeches buoy.

That Thursday night, as the *Sidonia* beat her way northwards out of gale-lashed St Andrews Bay, the steamer *London* was approaching the Tay at the end of her regular run from London to Dundee with passengers and goods. Her master, Captain Rattray, recalled later that the weather had worsened steadily as he came north until he too was in the grip of the same gale which had beset the *Sidonia*.

Just after 10.30 p.m., while lining up the Buddon lights before entering the river, Rattray saw a rocket fired from the direction of the Abertay Sands. *London* had just passed the fairway buoy about thirty minutes later when he saw a blue light flashed three times in five minutes, again from the direction of the Abertay Sands. Rattray knew that hazarding his own ship by closing the banks to respond to what were clearly distress signals would have been irresponsible in the extreme. He was, in any case, contending with difficulties of his own. The huge seas on the Tay Bar had carried away part of *London*'s upperworks and smashed a number of windows, flooding several cabins and the pantry. One passenger was washed into the lee scuppers and narrowly escaped being swept overboard.

Having got his battered command into Dundee, Rattray sent Harbourmaster John Jack a message that he believed there was a vessel in trouble on the banks and Jack despatched the steam tug *Hercules* to Broughty Ferry to pick up the lifeboat. The *Mary Hartley* was launched just after 3.00 a.m. and towed down to the river entrance. In the south-easterly gale, driving rain and pitch darkness, no trace of a vessel in distress could be seen and Coxswain George Anderson had the lifeboat towed back to sheltered water at Buddon to await daylight.

At first light, the *David and John,* a small schooner bound from Grangemouth to Montrose with a cargo of coal, was sighted at anchor in a dangerous position close to the Gaa Sands. *Hercules* could not close the banks so Anderson and his crew had to row for over a mile through mountainous seas. They got alongside the *David and John* and took off her crew of four shortly before the schooner struck the bank and broke up.

At 10.30 a.m., as the *Mary Hartley* arrived back at Broughty Ferry with the survivors from the *David and John,* millwright John Turnbull was about to leave Kinshaldy Farm near Leuchars. Just then, a shepherd ran into the farmyard shouting that there was a body and wreckage lying on the beach. Turnbull rode down to the shore where he discovered

A contemporary engraving depicting the Mary Hartley *crossing the Abertay Sands to the wreck of the* Dalhousie.

the shattered remains of a ship's boat. Close by, he found the sodden body of a man clad in a lifejacket lying face down in the sand. Beyond that, strewn along the water's edge, lay a trail of deck furniture, casks, chests and other luggage. Among the debris was another body, this time wearing two lifejackets on which Turnbull could read the words DALHOUSIE, DUNDEE.

At 11.00 a.m., as Turnbull continued his melancholy journey along Kinshaldy Beach, the steamer *Queen* arrived at Broughty Ferry with the news that her crew had seen the masts of a sunken ship on the south side of the banks. The *Mary Hartley* was immediately manned, this time under Coxswain John Knight, and towed down river by the *Queen*. Though many of the 13 crew aboard the lifeboat were fresh men, some, including both John Knight and George Anderson, had been out all night to the *David and John*. They had barely had time to get dry clothes and some hot food before the lifeboat put out for her second service.

Queen towed the *Mary Hartley* to no.6 buoy from where John Knight and his crew could clearly see two masts among the breakers some distance away to the south. Knight and Anderson knew that some of the wrecked ship's crew might still be alive, clinging desperately to the rigging, and resolved on the fastest route to the wreck. This meant pulling the *Mary Hartley* through the enormous, confused seas sweeping over the Abertay Sands. In a masterpiece of understatement, John Knight recorded in his service return that. 'The boat behaved admirably and was severely handled. When crossing the banks, the boat repeatedly filled.' A credit to her designer, her builders and her crew, the lifeboat battled on to reach the wreck site at about 2.00 p.m. The *Dalhousie*'s masts stood erect and seemingly oblivious to the seas sweeping past towards the shore. A sail flapped eerily from the mainmast but not a living soul could be seen.

Dalhousie had been built by Gourlay Brothers of Dundee for the Dundee and Newcastle Steam Shipping Company. At her trials in St Andrews Bay in April 1861, the 156 ton vessel was described as 'A rakish looking little steamer.' Despite being just 29 at the time, Henry Glenny had been given the command of the *Dalhousie* from new. A popular man who had begun his career as an ordinary seaman, he was known for driving his ship hard. In August 1861 the *Dalhousie* broke down off St Abbs Head and, after failing to make the Tay under sail, Glenny ran her aground off Arbroath. He had been fined 3/- (15p) for speeding on the Tyne in 1863, and, one night in October 1864, a month before the *Dalhousie* was lost, he had run down an Eyemouth trawler which sank with the loss of four of her six crew.

Dalhousie had been expected in Dundee at around the same time as the *London*. At first it was thought that Glenny might have elected to lie off until daylight, but, when there was no sign of her on the Friday morning, fears for the ship's safety grew. The first definite news reached Dundee when a shipping agent named Inglis travelled to Tayport that afternoon. According to the *Dundee Advertiser*, 'Fears for the vessel's safety were but too cruelly confirmed when . . . Mr Inglis was met by a cart containing two bodies.' The bodies were those found that morning by John Turnbull and Inglis was able to identify them as Captain Glenny and Tom Bisset, a seaman from Broughty Ferry.

The *Dalhousie*'s entire complement of 22 passengers and 12 crew were lost on that terrible night. A number of bodies were washed up over the weekend but it was clear that the women and children would probably have been below at the time of the sinking and would only be recovered by divers. The gale had subsided by the Tuesday and the tug *Rob Roy* sailed from Tayport carrying the North British Railway Company's diver George Watson. Watson's first attempts to gain access to the main saloon were thwarted by deck cargo which had fallen down companionways. On Wednesday, however, he found his way into the cabin through the skylight. Climbing down, his feet landed on the large, round table through the centre of which passed the mainmast.

He was immediately struck how well ordered the cabin still appeared; even the mirror fixed to the mast was still in place. Once his eyes became accustomed to the gloom, he saw two children, both girls, huddled together on a settee. A woman was jammed behind the stove with the body of young boy held tightly in her arms and another woman had her arm thrust through a gap in the deck planking. When the bodies were landed at Tayport, it was discovered that the woman holding the boy was Mrs Cowperthwaite, the wife of the engineer of the *Rob Roy*. The other bodies were those of Marian Strang and her three children. Mrs Strang and her husband were a well-known stage duo on their way to fulfil an engagement in Dundee. Scattered among the debris on the beach were theatrical costumes and pages of sheet music.

The exact cause of the loss of the *Dalhousie*, the worst shipping disaster to strike the River Tay, will remain a mystery. The most likely explanation is that, while approaching the Tay Bar, she was struck by a particularly large wave that somehow disabled her engine. Probably with the assistance of the male passengers, the crew then hoisted sail and Glenny attempted to run his ship ashore as far south of the banks as possible. He would have seen the lights of the *London* as she made her way up river but, as he made his distress signals, would have known that she was powerless to assist. The last moments in the main saloon, as the two women tried to comfort the children while the sea burst hungrily in, can only have been truly terrifying.

The *Mary Hartley* was launched again five days after the *Dalhousie* disaster when a Prussian galliot, the *Hercules,* inbound from Stettin with wheat, was reported in a dangerous position off Carnoustie. In the event, the lifeboat's services were not required as the Prussian managed to sail out of trouble.

While the crew of the *Mary Hartley* enjoyed richly-deserved public acclaim following their 'gallant exertions' in going out to the wrecks of the *David and John* and the *Dalhousie,* it was clear that all was not well with the management of the St Andrews lifeboat. Coxswain Mackrell's unaccountable refusal to accept that the *Sidonia* was flying a distress signal had attracted much adverse comment, as had the muddle over the sending of the lifeboat to the wreck of the *Napoleon* at Boarhills. Matters came to a head at the end of December when an exercise launch developed into an ugly confrontation with the crew refusing Mackrell's request that they man the boat. Mackrell stood down and was replaced by fisherman Tom Melville.

The case of the *Napoleon* had also exposed one of the major shortcomings of St Andrews as a lifeboat station. Launching from a beach exposed to the full fury of an easterly gale was always difficult and dangerous, occasionally even impossible. Once afloat, the lifeboat was then faced with a long row into the wind to reach a wreck on the rocky coastline east of the town. There was a clear case for a lifeboat to be stationed where, in an easterly, she would be to windward of any vessel in distress.

George Bruce, a member of the St Andrews Lifeboat Committee, did not share Purvis and Mackrell's view that the creek used by fishermen at Boarhills was unsuitable for lifeboat operations. After much protracted wrangling, he managed to buy the old *Volunteer Lifeboat* and had her boatshed at the Swilcan Burn taken down and carted, stone by stone, to Boarhills. There it was rebuilt and the *Volunteer Lifeboat,* renamed *Bruce's Own,* took up her new station in December 1865.

The *Mary Hartley* was launched at 9.00 a.m. on Wednesday, 8 February 1865, in response to the firing of the signal cannon at Buddon Ness. The North British Railway Company's steamer *Rob Roy* put out from Tayport and towed the lifeboat down river to the timber ship *Anja* which was lying at anchor among the breakers on the Abertay Sands. The *Mary Hartley* put a line aboard the *Anja* and she was towed to safety. Heavy seas were still breaking on the banks the following morning when the *Mary Hartley* was again towed down river by the *Rob Roy.* The Dundee schooner *Margaret* had gone ashore on the Abertay Sands at 3.00 a.m. while outbound in ballast. The *Margaret's* crew were taken off and the *Mary Hartley* was back on station by 11.00 a.m.

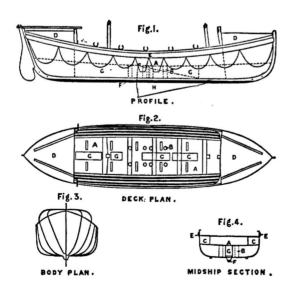

SELF-RIGHTING LIFEBOAT

A – Represents the deck.

B – Relieving valves for the automatic discharge of water off the deck.

C – Side air-cases above deck.

D – End air-compartments, usually called "end-boxes," an important factor in "self-righting."

E – The "wale" or "fender".

F – Iron keel ballast, important in general stability and self-righting.

G – Water-ballast tanks.

H – Drop-keels.

Less than a week after the service to the *Margaret*, Dundee Harbour Trust agreed to subscribe £50 towards the cost of installing an electric telegraph between the Buddon lights and the dock office in Dundee. The balance of the cost, almost £200, was raised by public subscription on the basis that the telegraph would be of great assistance to the lifeboat. The Harbour Trustees were, no doubt, delighted to be gaining a valuable aid to the pilotage service at a fraction of its true cost!

That the new telegraph did little to assist lifeboat operations can be seen from the fact that the signal guns remained in use for many years after its installation. The Buddon Ness signal gun was heard at 12.30 p.m. on Wednesday, 6 December 1865 when the jute-laden schooner *Princess* of Arbroath was wrecked on the Abertay Sands. Coxswain John Knight launched the *Mary Hartley* within five minutes of the gun and pulled round to Broughty Harbour to seek a tow from one of the railway steamers. The *Thane of Fife* had steam up but her master refused to help as a passenger train was due from Dundee. The other passenger ferry, *Auld Reekie,* had passengers aboard and was also unwilling to assist. Only Captain Milne of the goods ferry *Carrier* would help, though 20 minutes had to be spent in removing wagons from her deck.

The *Princess* was found well up on the bank with her crew of five having taken to the rigging. She was smashed to pieces by the breaking surf just as the *Mary Hartley* cast off from the *Carrier.* Helped by the fishing yawl *Peggy,* the lifeboat carried out a fruitless search for survivors. Much public indignation was directed towards the masters of the passenger ferries.

There was only one effective service for the *Mary Hartley* in 1866 when, just before 9.00 a.m. on 30 November, the Dundee schooner *Tay* was wrecked on the Gaa Sands. Captain Gibb had completely missed the entrance to the channel in early morning haze and ran aground among the shoals in the Gaa Lake. The lifeboat was launched at 9.30 a.m. and towed down to the banks by the *Auld Reekie*. She was pulled through the surf to rescue the *Tay*'s crew of five.

Chapter Five

EXERTED THEMSELVES TO THE UTMOST

The *Princess* service in 1866 had highlighted once again the difficulties faced by a pulling and sailing lifeboat based at Broughty Ferry in reaching a vessel stranded on the banks in an easterly gale. This led to the re-opening of the Buddon Ness lifeboat station in March 1867. The new Buddon lifeboat was the experimental iron self-righter *Eleanora* built in 1863 by Hepworth of Millwall and first stationed at Teignmouth in Devon.

As she had been paid for out of funds raised in the British settlements at Hong Kong and Shanghai, while at Teignmouth she was named *China*. An iron boat was found to be too heavy for launching across Teignmouth beach and, in 1864, she was transferred to New Brighton as the *Willie and Arthur*. Here, she was kept afloat on a mooring but, at 33 feet long, she was too small. As the *Eleanora,* she was transferred to Buddon Ness station in 1867. A new shed was constructed ashore to house the boarding boat and other gear.

The *Mary Hartley* was replaced by another boat bearing the same name in August 1867 after the timbers of the original were found to be badly rotted. The second *Mary Hartley* carried out her first service on Saturday, 24 October 1868 when the barque *Betty and Louise* of Hamburg stranded on the south side of the Abertay Sands. Captain Holm was bound for Burntisland and thought he was entering the Forth. Two signal guns were fired from St Andrews after he was seen standing into danger. Realising his mistake, Holm bore away to the north-east but soon found himself in broken water south of the Abertay Sands and anchored.

The tide was ebbing and, by 3.00 p.m., the *Betty and Louise* was striking the bottom. She began to make water and Holm's crew were getting their longboat ready when, at 5.00 p.m., they saw the *Mary Hartley* coming down river in tow of the steamer *Napier*. The lifeboat had been launched in response to a telegram sent from St Andrews even before the *Betty and Louise* struck, and was rowed across the Abertay Sands to take the nine crewmen off the sinking barque. Broughty Ferry fishermen salvaged the *Betty and Louise* the following day and were each awarded a share of £45 for their trouble.

St Andrews lifeboat station had clearly put its troubles behind it when, on a dark and wet night at the beginning of December 1867, the *Annie* was launched to the aid of the Fraserburgh sloop *Christian and Charlotte* which had been driven onto the Burnstools by an north-easterly gale. A pilot boat tried to get to her but was forced back by heavy seas and the signal guns were fired to summon the lifeboat crew. Captain James Mackay and his three crew had only just been brought ashore when the *Christian and Charlotte* broke up.

Both the St Andrews and the Boarhills lifeboats were launched at the end of October 1868 when the Norwegian brig *Oscar* ran ashore between St Andrews Castle and Lady Melville's Cave. The crew of the *Bruce's Own* included Coxswain Willie Chisholm and his three sons. Coxswain Tom Melville and his three sons were among the crew of *Annie* who saved the *Oscar's* crew of eight. This would appear to have been Willie Chisholm's last lifeboat service as he died in January 1871.

Two months after the service to the *Oscar,* the *Annie* guided the Scarborough smack *Canton* safely into harbour. In October 1870 she landed the crew of the schooner *Let* which had run ashore on the West Sands and, a month later, she stood by nine fishing boats struggling to get into harbour in a gale. The *Annie* was renamed *Polly and Lucy* in 1871 and undertook her last service on the morning of 23 January 1872. She was launched at 9.00 a.m. after the Norwegian schooner *Oal*, bound for Leith from Antwerp in ballast, was seen in difficulties in the bay. Lifeboatmen John Fenton and Dan Wilson were put aboard the schooner to help bring her safely into harbour. The new St Andrews lifeboat *Ladies Own* was presented to the station by the Newark Lifeboat Fund in 1873.

The sandbanks at the mouth of the Tay are constantly shifting and, despite the efforts of dredgers, the Buddon lights were not always directly in line with the channel. Captain Robert

Reece of the three masted schooner *No.4* was unable to find a pilot to help him into Dundee on 26 January 1873. Referring to Pearson's Nautical Almanac, he read that the channel had moved slightly west of the line of the leading lights at Buddon and steered his ship accordingly. He had the low light open a little east of the high light when the schooner grounded suddenly on the Elbow End and began pounding heavily. Captain Reece and his men were clearing away their longboat when one of the crew fell overboard. Reece and one other man jumped into the longboat to rescue the fallen sailor but the line holding them to the schooner parted and they were carried across the river to land on the Gaa Sands. Reece walked to Buddon from where the lightkeeper telegraphed to Broughty Ferry for the lifeboat.

The *Mary Hartley* was launched at 5.45 a.m. and, as no steamers were available at that early hour, set off down river under oars. She was overtaken by Charles Norrie's fishing boat taking fishermen to man the *Eleanora* at Buddon. The *Eleanora* was already under way with five pilots at the oars when Norrie arrived and put eight men aboard her. Tom Liddle, the mate of the *No. 4,* recalled seeing the pilot cutter and the *Eleanora* standing by but unable to get close as there was insufficient water on the banks. The *Mary Hartley* arrived and attempted to close the wrecked schooner but grounded repeatedly. Coxswain Anderson decided to go round the tail of the bank and approach the wreck from the south. They had only gone part of the way when the schooner, which was being struck by ever larger seas as the tide rose, broke up. Liddle and two seamen were saved when the *Eleanora* made a daring swoop into the breakers to pluck them from the remains of the poop deck to which they had lashed themselves. Three other seamen were washed ashore, clinging to pieces of wreckage, at Buddon Ness.

Captain Reece had little time to celebrate his survival before Dundee Harbourmaster Captain William Robertson carted him off to see an optician. Poor eyesight was not the cause of the sinking, however, and Robertson later reported that it was due to a combination of the lamentable state of the pilotage service and misleading instructions in Pearson's Almanac. This roused publisher George Pearson to a strongly worded letter of protest. He pointed out that the Fraternity of Masters and Seamen had failed to notify him of changes in bearings at the river entrance. Management of the lighting and buoyage on the river was brought under the control of the Harbour Trust by the Harbour Consolidation Act of 1875. Pilotage also came under the trustees' control though shipmasters were not then compelled to use a pilot.

The St Andrews lifeboat *Ladies Own* rescued the six crew of the Norwegian schooner *Anna* after her anchor cable parted in a gale and she drifted ashore onto the East Sands near Gibson's Road on 12 May 1874. That October, the *Bruce's Own* was able to help earn her keep by offering trips around the Royal Navy's Channel Fleet at anchor in the Bay.

Another schooner, the *Ward Jackson* of Carnarvon, was seen wallowing in the breakers south of the Abertay Sands on the morning of 25 February 1875 after her Captain, John Jones, somehow mistook the Buddon Lights for the the Isle of May Light. Captain Packham of the outbound D.P.&L. steamer *London* put back up the river and fired two guns as a signal to the fishermen. The *Mary Hartley* was launched at 8.00 a.m. and towed down river by the *London*. The *Ward Jackson* had sunk when they reached the banks and George Anderson had to rescue her crew of five from the rigging. The strong ebb tide meant that Anderson had to bring the lifeboat back through The Pool, reaching Broughty Ferry by 10.00 a.m.

A strong easterly gale was still blowing the following afternoon as the steamer *Tuskar* went down river at the start of her regular run between Dundee and Liverpool. *Tuskar* reached no. 3 buoy at 7.30 p.m. but Captain Lawson decided that the weather was too bad for him to put to sea. He tried to turn the *Tuskar* in the channel but she was driven back onto the Abertay Sands and, as she rolled to and fro in the surf, her distress signals were seen at Carnoustie, Buddon Ness and St Andrews.

Coxswain John Knight launched the *Mary Hartley* at 8.00 p.m. and set off down river under oars. She made little headway into the teeth of the gale but was soon overtaken by the steamer *Thane of Fife* and towed out to the banks. Another crew went down to man the *Eleanora*, rocket brigades at St Andrews and Carnoustie were alerted and the *Ladies Own* was launched from the mouth of the Eden. The Arbroath lifeboat *People's Friend No.2* set out by road but was not needed and turned back at Elliot.

The *Eleanora* and the *Mary Hartley* had to wait until midnight before there was enough water on the banks for them to approach the stranded steamer. The *Mary Hartley* went alongside first and took off 16 survivors, breaking three oars in the process. Her return to Broughty Ferry was greeted by the 'hearty acclamations' of a large crowd waiting on Fisher Street and the pilot pier. The *Eleanora* went alongside a little while later to take off Captain Lawson and the remaining five crewmen. The *Tuskar* was refloated at high water the following day, though the masters of the two tugs involved had a bitter dispute over their respective salvage claims.

The *Mary Hartley* was back at the banks early on Saturday, 25 September 1875, when distress signals were seen coming from a stranded brig which turned out to be the timber-laden *Catherina* of Riga. She had been carried west of the channel and into shoal water in heavy weather the previous evening. Her crew had spent the night in the rigging before being rescued by the lifeboat. The *Catherina* was later refloated and brought into the river through The Pool.

Less than a month later, in a strong easterly gale and driving rain on 18 October, Captain Strenga of the Riga registered schooner *Leopold* was approaching what he firmly believed was the Tyne. Too late, he realised that St Andrews was not, in fact, Whitby and he was left with no option but to run his ship ashore close to The Pool. The *Mary Hartley* was towed down river by the steamer *Star o' Tay* and guided the *Leopold* through The Pool into sheltered water. Strong easterlies were still blowing four days later, on 22 October, when the Tayport bound brig *Vidar* was swept broadside onto the banks. Captain Sorensen had been forced to attempt the river on his own as the pilot cutter was nowhere to be seen. Sorensen and his seven crewmen were taken off by the *Mary Hartley* early the following morning.

The *Mary Hartley*'s last service launch took place on 2 November 1875 when she stood by the schooner *Maria* of Goole until she got clear of the banks. In her nine years on station she had been launched on service 16 times, saving 52 lives. Similar in design to her predecessor, the new Broughty Ferry lifeboat had been presented by the readers of the *English Mechanic and World of Science* magazine. She arrived in Dundee on Monday, 5 June 1876, and was taken in procession through the city to the harbour. The *Dundee Advertiser* recorded the scene;

> The boat, placed on its cradle and fully manned (each member of the crew having on a lifebelt and red nightcap - the coxswains, George Anderson and John Knight, being in their places at the stern), with her masts rigged, the mainmast bearing the flag of the Royal National Lifeboat Institution, presented a gay and attractive appearance. Shortly after eleven o'clock the procession left the West Railway Station. In front was the band of the *Mars*; then a number of the boys; afterwards a few of the men of the *Unicorn*; next the boat drawn by six splendid horses of the Caledonian Railway Company; and lastly an open carriage, in which were seated Mr Yeaman MP; Bailie Edward; and Mr James Hunter, the Secretary of the Local Branch of the Lifeboat Institution. The route was by Union Street, Nethergate, Tay Street, Ward Road, round the Albert Institute, along Reform and Castle Streets to the north side of King William's [sic] Dock. All the way the streets were densely crowded, and at the place of launch there was an immense assemblage, men and boys being perched on every conceivable elevation from which a view of the proceedings might be obtained.
>
> A suitable prayer having been offered by the Rev. Dr Watson, the order was given to proceed with the launch. Mrs Dalgleish having broken the bottle, named the boat *English Mechanic* and expressed the hope that God's blessing might attend her. In a few seconds afterwards the lifeboat was plunged into the dock, and two or three of the crew seated in the bow were slightly drenched.

The *English Mechanic* was craned over for her self-righting demonstration, turning upright and draining in 25 seconds. Members of the committee then boarded the steamer *Fairweather* to follow the lifeboat down river for her sea trials. A stiff westerly breeze was speeding the *English Mechanic* past Broughty Ferry under canvas when the *Fairweather* steamed alongside with the news that a schooner was flying a distress signal close to the Gaa Sands. *Fairweather* took the lifeboat in tow and and made for the disabled vessel which turned out to be the *Brothers* of Newcastle, inbound for Dundee with a cargo of cement. Five of the lifeboat crew

LIGHTSHIP

FOR THE

RIVER TAY.

NOTICE TO MARINERS.

The TRUSTEES of the HARBOUR of DUNDEE hereby GIVE NOTICE that, on or about 15th OCTOBER, 1877, a LIGHT VESSEL will be moored near the ENTRANCE of the RIVER TAY, and opposite the ABERTAY SPIT, with the following Bearings and Distances, viz. :—

2 Miles S.E.⅓S. from Buddonness High Light Tower;

6½ Miles E.S.E from Tayport Lights; and

2 miles N.W.⅓N. from the Fairway Buoy.

5 Cable Lengths N.E. from the Elbow End.

2 Cable Lengths W.N.W. from No. 3 Red Buoy on the Gaa Sands.

The Lightship will ride in 5½ Fathoms at Low Water. She will exhibit from her Foremast, from sunset to sunrise, a **FLASHING WHITE LIGHT** every Ten Seconds, which will be visible in clear weather about 8 miles distant. During foggy weather a Bell will be rung.

The Light Vessel will have two masts, and be painted Red, with the word " ABERTAY " in White Letters on her sides.

WILLIAM THOMS,
Clerk to Harbour Trustees.

HARBOUR CHAMBERS,
DUNDEE, 10th October, 1877.

D. R. CLARK & SON, PRINTERS, CASTLE STREET, DUNDEE

were put aboard the schooner but found her sails and rigging badly damaged and her pumps not working. *Fairweather* towed the schooner up to Dundee and a large crowd cheered the *English Mechanic* into Broughty Ferry after she had been delivered, named and out on her first service, all in one day!

The news that another schooner was aground near the Elbow End arrived by telegram at the Dock Office in Dundee at 9.00 a.m. on 4 September 1876. Another telegram arrived shortly afterwards from Buddon Ness which said that two schooners were ashore on the Abertay Sands and another was anchored in a dangerous position in shoal water south of the bank. The

The first Abertay lightship was placed on station on 15 October 1877. The lightship was built by James Roney at Arbroath and, for over 60 years, her bright single flash every ten seconds was a reassuring sight to shipmasters using the river. She survived near-destruction in a storm in January 1937 and was replaced two years later by a steel vessel built in the Caledon Shipyard. The old lightship ended her days as a wartime blockship.

(DUNDEE COURIER AND EVENING TELEGRAPH)

steamers *Flying Scotsman, May* and *Gazelle* were despatched down river, picking up the *English Mechanic* on the way.

They first came across the schooner *Emerald* of Montrose, inbound for Dundee with a cargo of moulding sand. The *Emerald* had struck at 8.30 a.m. after mistaking a small schooner for the pilot cutter. Not far away lay the stranded Norwegian schooner *Aristide*. Bound for Perth with timber, she had gone ashore at 6.30 a.m. and it was her distress flag that Captain Dempster of the *Emerald* had mistaken for the pilot flag. The *English Mechanic* made several attempts to get alongside the sinking *Aristide* but grounded repeatedly and broke four oars. The schooner's crew were picked up by Robert Ferrier's fishing boat as the lifeboat crew struggled in the breakers.

The third schooner anchored in the shoals south of the Abertay Sands turned out to be the Russian *Magdalene*. Her master had been following the *Emerald* and had seen her come to grief in time to drop anchor. She was taken in tow by the tug *May* and brought up to anchor in Broughty Ferry Roads. Both the *Emerald* and the *Aristide* were later refloated and repaired.

Another double service for the *English Mechanic* began when wreckage was washed ashore at the mouth of the Tay in a south-easterly storm on 3 December 1876. The lifeboat searched the banks but no sign was ever found of the five crew of the Norwegian brig *Felicie*, bound for the Baltic from Alloa in ballast. The *English Mechanic* was launched again at daybreak the following day in response to a report from Captain Johnstone of the SS *Scotia* that a ship was anchored in a perilous position near the Banks. The lifeboat was towed out by the tug *Fairweather* and stood by as the German brig *Antje* was taken in tow by the steamer *May*.

The Norwegian *Alma* of Drammen, bound for the Forth with timber, ran ashore on the

Abertay Sands late on 4 October 1877 after her master had mistaken Fife Ness for St Abbs Head. Four of her crew left in a small boat to summon help and were picked up by the steam collier *Neilson Taylor* at around 1.00 a.m. on the 5th. Both the *English Mechanic* and the *Eleanora* stood by as the master of the *Alma* struck a deal with the master of the tug *Flying Scotsman* at £100 for a tow clear of the bank.

The *English Mechanic* did not play any part in the search for bodies that followed the collapse of the first Tay Bridge in a storm at 7.15 p.m. on Sunday, 28 December 1879, just over 18 months after it had opened. A passenger train bound from Burntisland to Dundee precipitated the disaster when it was derailed after running over a twisted rail in the 'High Girders' section over the navigation channel. The flimsy, shoddily constructed bridge simply fell apart and all 75 passengers and crew on the north-bound train were killed. The train ferry between Broughty Ferry and Tayport, closed on the opening of the bridge in May 1878, enjoyed a new lease of life though plans for a new bridge were well in hand by November 1880.

Captain Andrew Baxter of the brigantine *Oscar* sailed from Dundee on the morning of 22 February 1881 with a cargo of yarn for the Spanish Mediterranean port of San Feliu de Guixols. *Oscar* left King William Dock at 8.15 a.m. in fine weather but, by the time she reached the Lady Buoy, the wind was freshening rapidly. She had not gone much further when the wind suddenly changed direction and drove her, helpless, onto the Abertay Sands. Buddon lifeboat, recently renamed *May,* took off seven men including the pilot. The *Oscar* broke up soon after her crew had left.

The first three months of 1881 were marked by the worst weather seen for many years. Twice the average rainfall fell in February and the first few days of March brought the worst snowstorms and gales since 1827. Some 30 vessels and 200 lives were lost between Fife Ness and Wick in the first days of March alone. The *English Mechanic* was launched at 5.15 p.m. on Friday 4 March when a schooner was seen ashore on the Lady Bank, two miles east of Broughty Ferry. No tug was available so the lifeboatmen had to pull through a south-easterly gale, heavy seas and blinding snow squalls to reach the Russian schooner *Niels*.

Coxswain George Anderson wrote, 'The crew exerted themselves to the utmost to rescue the crew [of the *Neils*] before it became totally dark and, after two hours hard pulling, got alongside and took off the crew, five in number, and landed them at Broughty Ferry shortly before 8.00 p.m.' Anderson's phlegmatic report does little to convey the difficulty of this service. The visibility was so bad that only the briefest glimpses of the wreck could be seen between heavy falls of snow and a man had to be stationed ashore with a powerful light to guide the lifeboat. The lifeboat came up heavily under the *Neils'* counter but was fortunately undamaged. Coxswain Anderson sailed her back to Broughty Ferry under a double-reefed foresail, all the canvas she could safely carry.

Heavy, driving snow was still falling the following afternoon when another schooner was seen being driven onto the West Sands in St Andrews. Thousands of spectators were attracted by the signal guns alerting the Rocket Brigade and the crew of the *Ladies Own*. The *Harmonie* of Mandal grounded on the West Sands 200 yards north of the Swilcan Burn and Captain Neilsen and his crew of four could be seen huddled near the stern. The *Ladies Own* pulled alongside after a brief struggle and they were brought safely ashore. The wreck had taken place during the middle of the annual Kate Kennedy procession and the survivors were taken aback when confronted by, amongst others, Rob Roy, Mephistopheles and Robin Hood.

Hardly had excitement over the wreck of the *Harmonie* subsided when the signal guns were fired again as another ship, this time a brigantine, was seen standing into the bay. She was heading straight for the rocks below St Andrews Castle but dropped anchor after a gun was fired to warn her of the danger. Both her anchor cables parted, however, and she crashed onto the rocks at 5.15 p.m. A rocket line was fired across the wreck but the stranded seamen had scarcely begun to haul in the whip when the wreck lurched over and the line parted.

For the second time that afternoon, the *Ladies Own* went out but, due to the heavy seas and the amount of floating wreckage barring their way, the lifeboat could get no nearer than 50 yards and the brigantine broke up, pitching her crew of eleven to their deaths in full view of the horrified spectators. The sea was blackened as 700 tons of small coal spilled out of her holds. A broken nameboard identified the wreck as the *Merlin* of Sunderland, Captain Griffith Lewis, bound for Bordeaux from Wearmouth*.

Rescue efforts were still in progress at the *Merlin* when coastguards at Carnoustie reported a brig steering an erratic course into the Tay past the Abertay lightship. The *Arabian* of Gravesend, she was bound from Gravesend for the Tyne in ballast. Having been blown north at the mercy of the gale, she was attempting to enter the river for shelter. Lacking both a pilot and local knowledge, Captain Wallace Bell did well to get as far as he did, but was finally driven ashore on the Lady Bank, close to the wreck of the *Neils*.

Fisher Street, Broughty Ferry at the end of the 19th century. This view has changed little in the ensuing 100 years though both the fisher folk and their boats have long-since disappeared. The boatshed built in 1862 to house the Mary Hartley *stands between the street and the river.*
(DUNDEE COURIER AND EVENING TELEGRAPH)

George Anderson launched the *English Mechanic* shortly after 5.00 p.m. and, for the second time in two days, his crew had to pull down river into a gale and driving snow. Despite appalling visibility, they found the *Arabian* lying 300 yards off Monifieth at 7.00 p.m. She was bumping heavily and making a great deal of water, but Captain Bell was determined to save his ship and refused all offers of help from the lifeboatmen.

The gale was still blowing hard two days later, on Monday, 7 March, when the *Ladies Own* and the *Bruce's Own*, the old 1824 *Volunteer Lifeboat* now stationed at Boarhills, were launched to another vessel in distress. The *Grasshopper* had come to anchor dangerously close to rocks off Boarhills after being battered by storms for 12 days. Her plight was reported by men searching for bodies from the wreck of the *Merlin*. The *Ladies Own* took off the *Grasshopper*'s crew of six who told the St Andrews lifeboatmen that they had earlier been hailed by a longboat containing nine survivors from yet another wreck. The *Bruce's Own*

---

* The nameboard survives and is displayed in the St Andrews Preservation Trust museum.

carried out a search but found nothing and *Grasshopper* was reboarded by her crew the following day, just before some local fishermen attempted salvage.

The longboat seen by the crew of the *Grasshopper* held the crew of the Norwegian brig *Oliver* which had been trapped close to the North Carr Rock at Fife Ness. News of the *Oliver*'s predicament reached Anstruther at about 9.00 a.m. on the Monday morning. Coxswain Martin Gardner and his crew set out for Fife Ness by road with the Anstruther lifeboat *Admiral Fitzroy* on her carriage pulled by a team of 4 horses.

Conditions on the road were terrible; the gale had backed to the north-east and was blowing with unremitting fury. It was bitterly cold and heavy falls of sleet and snow had covered the road with mud and slush. Twelve horses had to be harnessed to the carriage before the *Admiral Fitzroy* reached the launch site at Balcomie. The sinking brig was found abandoned and the *Admiral Fitzroy* returned to Anstruther at 4.00 p.m. after a lengthy but fruitless search for her crew. Two hours later, a St Monans fishing boat came into Anstruther Harbour with the nine frozen Norwegians on board.

The *Ladies Own* took the crew off the Norwegian schooner *Frederickstadt* in the early hours of Tuesday, 25 October 1881. Bound for Newcastle with a cargo of barrel staves, she had run ashore on the West Sands after her anchor cable parted in an easterly gale. The lifeboat was struck by several heavy seas but returned ashore with five survivors.

By 1881, after almost 60 years, the old *Volunteer Lifeboat* had finally come to the end of her useful life and the new Boarhills lifeboat *John and James Mills* left David Livie's Dundee shipyard* on the day after the wreck of the *Frederickstadt*. The new 31 foot self-righting boat was taken to St Andrews by road the following day and launched from the East Sands before being towed to Boarhills. The station at Boarhills remained outwith the RNLI and the new boat, which, along with her carriage, cost £700, was paid for by the Dundee businessmen after whom she was named. The boatshed at Boarhills was enlarged and the floor was concreted to take the new boat.

The *English Mechanic* and the *May* were both manned on the morning of 4 November 1881 when the French lugger *Francois Marie*, Dundee bound from Kings Lynn with coprolites, went ashore in worsening weather on the Abertay Sands. The *English Mechanic* was towed down by the tug *Iron King*. The *May* took off five of the lugger's crew but the ship's boy aged 13 was picked up dead and was buried in Barnhill Cemetery.

St Andrews lifeboat saved the four crew of the Arbroath-bound coal schooner *Rosebud* which went ashore near the mouth of the Eden on 2 February 1883. Just over two years later, on 9 April 1885, the *Ladies Own* under Coxswain Peter Waters stood by the fishing boat *Pride o' the Ocean* which got into trouble in the Bay while being sailed back from Lerwick by the owner's son and two other lads.

Dundee's first telephone exchange had opened in India Buildings in January 1880. Within four years, 330 subscribers had signed up for 'telephone privileges' at an average annual cost of £5. 10/- (£5.50). A telephone had been installed at Buddon Ness when, on 15 March 1888, the lightkeeper rang the Dundee Harbourmaster, Captain Yule, to tell him of two vessels riding to their anchors in an easterly gale off the river entrance.

The *English Mechanic* was launched at 1.00 p.m. and towed out by the tug *Fairweather*. She had only reached the Horsehoe Buoy when, through heavy snow, her crew saw two three-masted schooners coming up river towards the Abertay lightship. The *Willem* of Harlingen, leading, was inbound for Dundee with a cargo of moss litter and her master had decided to attempt the river without a pilot after catching a glimpse of the lightship through the snow. The second ship, the *Queen of the Mistley* of Harwich, had been drifting about in the North Sea for almost two weeks, totally at the mercy of the weather. As she followed the *Willem* over The

---

* David Livie remained in business in Dundee until his death, aged 70, in 1920. An internationally renowned, award-winning boatbuilder, in addition to the private Boarhills lifeboat, he constructed a number of lifeboats for the RNLI. His customers also included the Royal Navy and the Russian government.

Bar, several huge seas broke over her, sweeping her after deckhouse and one of her boats over the side. The lifeboat and the tug stood by both vessels until they were safely into sheltered water.

Chapter Six

ARE YE A' READY NOO, CHAPS?

Second item on the agenda for the Broughty Ferry Burgh Magistrates meeting on Monday, 11 June 1888, was a letter from Alexander Mitchelson, Secretary of the Dundee Branch of the Ancient Order of Foresters. Mitchelson sought permission to erect a platform on Beach Crescent for the launching and naming ceremony of the new Broughty Ferry lifeboat presented by the Order. The request was granted and the Superintendent of Police was instructed to make arrangements for public safety. As they moved on to discuss weightier matters such as the adulteration of milk and scavenger's wages, the Magistrates could have had little idea of what they were letting themselves in for.

The Foresters gathered together members of various different friendly societies from as far afield as America and, on Saturday, 23 June, a vast procession formed up on Dundee Esplanade. Many of the marchers wore the traditional costume of their order; two Foresters from Denny wore clothes made from bear and fox skins and Brother Scott from Massachusetts was handsomely attired as a Knight of Sherwood Forest. Two Dundee Foresters cut a dash in yellow boots, buckskin trousers, dark green coats trimmed with ermine and broad green hats topped with white feathers.

Almost 15,000 people assembled at Beach Crescent, Broughty Ferry, on the evening of Saturday, 23 June 1888, for the naming ceremony of the Samuel Shawcross. *A rather harassed stationmaster reported that Broughty Ferry railway station had issued 4,334 tickets on that quite extraordinary day.*
(DUNDEE ART GALLERIES AND MUSEUMS)

At the head of this colourful procession, mounted on her carriage drawn by a team of eight horses, was the new lifeboat. Designed by the RNLI's new consulting naval architect, G.L. Watson, and built in the Glasgow yard of D.& W. Henderson & Co., she was 37 feet long, fully self righting and equipped for both sailing and pulling by 12 oarsmen.

The *Dundee Advertiser* takes up the story;

Shortly before four o'clock a bugle sounded and a few minutes later the bands began to play, and the procession moved off amid loud cheers from the spectators, several thousands in number, who lined the Esplanade. Mr Mann, the Chief Marshal, led the way in front of the lifeboat, which had the Union Jack at its prow, the national ensign at the stern and the flag of the National Lifeboat Institution in the centre. The route was by Union Street, Nethergate, High Street, Reform Street, Meadowside, Commercial Street and Dock Street to Broughty Ferry. The procession was about a mile in length and consisted of fully 2,500 members. Along a considerable part of the route, the roadway was lined with spectators who manifested considerable interest in the novel procession. The walk to Broughty Ferry, about four miles distant, took upwards of an hour.

Led by the pipers of the Pride of Tay Lodge of Shepherds and the Arbroath Artillery brass band, yet another parade left Broughty Ferry and joined the main procession coming from Dundee at Harecraigs. The *Advertiser*'s coverage of this extraordinary event continues;

Never before was there seen such an immense multitude in Broughty Ferry. The gigantic train of processionists filed along Beach Crescent and took up positions in the street and on the beach. The inhabitants of Broughty Ferry turned out en masse, while thousands of visitors were present, many arriving by railway and others accompanying the processionists on foot from Dundee. In a short time after their arrival, Beach Crescent was crowded from end to end and the beach in front of it down to the water's edge was densely packed, the railway and harbour piers on either side were covered with a solid mass, a flotilla of boats filled the harbour, while high on the house tops overlooking were groups of interested spectators. The numbers present were variously estimated at from twelve to fifteen thousand.

Brother Lawrence Fargie, a senior Forester, said, 'Men of Broughty Ferry, it is ours in the providence of God to present this boat, but it is yours to supply the essential crew and, as the old boat which it now replaces has never been found wanting in that respect, we believe that the characteristic heroism of the past, when life was in danger, will still be displayed.'

RNLB Samuel Shawcross
(ROYAL NATIONAL LIFEBOAT INSTITUTION)

The speeches over, Fargie's daughter named the boat *Samuel Shawcross* after a prominent secretary of the Order of Foresters. With Coxswain James Ross at the helm, and to the accompaniment of loud cheering, the firing of guns and the Arbroath Artillery Band playing *The Boatie Rows,* she was launched and pulled out into the river.

Jack the Ripper was terrorising London's east end and Kier Hardie's Scottish Labour Party was being formed when, on 10 November 1888, the *Samuel Shawcross* was launched on service for the first time. Three vessels were seen embayed in an easterly gale from the coastguard station at Westhaven, Carnoustie, and a telegram was sent to the Dock Office at Dundee which arrived at 9.00 a.m. The tugs *Protector* and *Duncan* were sent down river, *Duncan* taking the lifeboat in tow as she passed Broughty Ferry. *Duncan* could get no further than the Abertay lightship due to the state of the tide and the enormous sea running on The Bar. The lifeboat put a river pilot aboard the *Viking,* bound for Montrose from Cronstadt, and stood by as she made her way into the river. About noon, the 102 year-old Norwegian barque *Sofia Maria* went ashore near the mouth of the Eden and the St Andrews lifeboat saved her crew of nine. Later that afternoon, the Danish brig *Boletta,* inbound from Memel for Granton with oak staves, struck the Gaa Sands and immediately broke up. Her crew got away in their own small boat just before the brig struck.

The barque *Elisabeth* of Tonsberg got into difficulties in St Andrews Bay while bound for Leith with pit props on 16 March 1891. Rockets were fired from St Andrews at 4.00 p.m. to warn her that she was standing into danger and she put about in an effort to get clear of the bay. Like so many ships before her, she was unable to get past Boarhills and put about again to run ashore on the West Sands at 7.00 p.m. With some of her oars double banked to get her through the surf, the St Andrews lifeboat was launched under Coxswain Alexander Greig at 7.20 p.m. and saved the *Elisabeth*'s crew of eight. A large crowd had assembled on the beach and there were loud cheers when the lifeboat came ashore with the survivors.

Another Norwegian vessel, the schooner *Fransis* of Drammen, was inbound for the Forth three weeks later, on 5 April, when she too was wrecked on the West Sands. The weather was so bad that the *Ladies Own* could not get off the beach and Coxswain James Gourlay and his crew set out to man the Boarhills lifeboat. The *John and James Mills* was able to launch from the narrow creek at Boarhills and rapidly bore down on the wreck of the *Fransis* to take off her crew of six. Despite the fact that Boarhills was a private lifeboat station, Jamie Gourlay was awarded the silver medal of the RNLI for this service and his crew were handsomely rewarded by the Norwegian Government.

The *John and James Mills* had been somewhat neglected and, when launched to the *Fransis,* leaked badly. She was repaired and a *St Andrews Citizen* reporter recorded the scene as Jamie Gourlay took his crew out on exercise in October 1891;

Arriving at the boathouse, we found everything neat and trig. On the boat being turned out, the crew handled her in a manner which showed how well-drilled and disciplined they are. They all act as smartly as if a ship were urgently in need of their services in the bay. Hardly a word is spoken. Each man has his allotted task, and he does it without bothering his neighbour. At last, everything is got ready; when, to give a touch of romance to the scene and show the interest the people in the village take in their boat, a number of comely Boarhills maidens, who have turned out to look on, give us a help to run the carriage down to the beach. This done we get on board along with the crew."Are ye a' ready noo chaps" shouts Jamie with the tiller already in his hand."Ay, ay," is the response by several of the crew."Now then, Captain," shouts Jamie to Captain Burn, "pull awa' as fast as ye like." There, there, there she goes, and the "sailor's friend" glides from her carriage and dips into the creek like a duck. Outside the beacon the sails are hoisted, and the crew begin to take notes of her sea-going qualities. A stiff breeze from the land carries us rapidly down the Bay, until when opposite old St Rule we turn about and tack for home.

The gallant little boat behaved beautifully. Her slight defect of April last having been removed, not a drop of water was drawn, and we reached the creek again after a very pleasant sail. Mounted once more on her carriage, Dr Hill's six horses were sent for, and soon the boat was safely in the boathouse again.

The RNLI had established Crail lifeboat station just four miles away at Fife Ness in 1884 and it was hard to keep up enthusiasm for Boarhills lifeboat when it was so rarely used. The station fell into disuse and the *John and James Mills* was left mouldering until August 1919 when she was sold in aid of the Shipwrecked Mariners Society. The boatshed, originally built next to the Swilcan Bridge in 1824, survives as a cattle shed.

The Broughty Ferry fishing fleet had reached a peak of more than 80 boats and 180 fishermen in the 1880s when the river and St Andrews Bay teemed with haddock, flounders and plaice. Shortly before 8.00 a.m. on Wednesday, 4 March 1891, a fleet of around 20 yawls left for the flounder fishing in St Andrews Bay. The day started fine with a moderate south-westerly breeze but, by late morning, the wind backed north-westerly and increased to gale force. From the shore, many of the fishing yawls could be seen in difficulties in rough seas and the *Samuel Shawcross* was launched at 4.15 p.m.

When the lifeboatmen reached the bay, they found all but two of the yawls were close inshore with the four larger ones anchored and the rest secured alongside them. Of the remaining two, Tom Gall's *Catherine* was at anchor some distance from the rest. The *Mary's* anchor rope parted but she reached the shore at Tentsmuir. One man jumped ashore but, such was the strength of the offshore wind, he found himself being dragged off the beach with the boat and was forced to let go. The boat began to drift rapidly out to sea with ex-Coxswain George Anderson still aboard. The lifeboat secured both the *Mary* and the *Catherine* and towed them up to Buddon Burn.

The yawl *Agnes and Ann* was caught by a north-easterly gale in the early hours of 23 August 1891 and tried unsuccessfully to run for shelter at Arbroath. St Andrews lifeboat was launched at 2.00 a.m. and put two men aboard the fishing boat before seeing her safely into harbour.

A number of Broughty Ferry yawls sailed on the morning of 15 December 1891 for the line fishing grounds west of the Bell Rock. Most of them had just shot their lines that evening when a south-easterly breeze suddenly freshened to a full gale accompanied by torrential rain and sleet. The fleet immediately hauled in their lines and made for the Tay but two boats, the *Osprey* and the *Grace* missed the river and ended up in St Andrews Bay. They put back out to sea and made the channel on the second attempt but, driven off course by strong cross currents in deteriorating visibility, the *Osprey* went hard aground on the Elbow End. Tom Norrie, skipper of the yawl *Jane Wedderburn*, reported the stranding then took his place at the oars in the *Samuel Shawcross*.

As in any human endeavour, things do, occasionally, go wrong. The unfortunate events as fishermen who were not part of the regular lifeboat crew attempted to man the boat were described in rather melodramatic terms by the *Broughty Ferry Guide and Carnoustie Gazette;*

> Instead of promptly launching the lifeboat, a rabble of fishermen argue with one another who is to man it. Lifebelts are torn off this one and put on another, while the language used would put Whitechapel to the blush. There is no cry of "For God's sake launch the boat and save our comrades!" The reverse is the case. What manhood, what love for dear life! At last, however, the regular crew of the boat turn up, and she starts on the the search for - many of them, we daresay, knew for what - a wreck and loss of life. And such was the result. There, on the bank opposite the Buddon lights, they discovered the poor Osprey completely covered with water and a total wreck.

A calamity such as the drowning of the five crew of the *Osprey* had a devastating effect in a small community like Broughty Ferry. In addition to the families of the dead men, it was also felt strongly by the lifeboatmen who were themselves fishermen and, more often than not, related to those lost. In the case of the *Osprey,* the youngest of Skipper William Cant's seven children had died the previous week and his brother, John Cant, left a family of eight. The body of the Cant's brother-in-law, John Lorimer, was found entangled in fishing gear in the bottom of the boat.

The *Samuel Shawcross* launched at 2.15 p.m. on 5 July 1893 after fishermen at the Castle Green saw the Harbour Trust steam tug *Princess Louise* run ashore on the Abertay Sands close to the wreck of the *Osprey. Princess Louise* had stranded while undertaking survey work. Another tug, the *Excelsior*, was close by towing pontoons with sand dredged from Tayport Harbour. She stopped and towed the *Princess Louise* off the bank before the lifeboat got there.

A violent gale blew up on Friday, 17 November 1893 and, by 10.00 p.m., it had increased to hurricane force. The sandboat *Union* was old and quite unable to make any headway against the storm. Captain Strachan anchored off Tayport and stayed at the helm, attempting to keep her head into the weather. The *Union* began to make water and sank, taking with her four crewmen who had refused to leave the warmth of the cabin. Strachan survived being pinned to the deck by an iron sand tub and swam ashore.

As the weather worsened that night, Captain Keith of the pilot cutter *No.2* became alarmed for the safety of his ship. He was preparing to seek shelter when she dragged her anchor, stranded on Abertay Sands and heeled over until broadside on to the gale on an ebbing tide. One witness wrote, 'Huge sheets of water swept the decks, the spray blew clean over the masthead and the crew were in imminent danger of being washed overboard.'

The cutter's crew took to the rigging, and as the hours passed, their position became ever more desperate. At daybreak, however, a distress rocket was sighted by fishermen at Broughty Ferry and the *Samuel Shawcross* was soon speeding down river under sail. She could not get close due to the sea conditions on the banks, so a line was passed and seven pilots were dragged to safety. Hundreds had gathered by the boatshed and a ringing cheer went up when they saw that the service had been successful. The sandboat *Union* was salvaged and, known to all as *The Hearse,* she soldiered on until 1904.

Working to windward. A yawl clearing the Tay Bar.
(SUSAN HUGHAN)

The Norwegian brig *Speculation* sailed from Tayport on the morning of Friday, 20 May 1898, bound for Bremen with a cargo of coal. She was going down river under the tow of a steam tug in a stiff breeze and choppy sea when the tow rope parted. A second line was passed but this too parted and, before anything could be done, the *Speculation* was driven onto the Abertay Sands. The stranding was seen from the shore and the *Samuel Shawcross* was launched. Seas were breaking over the brig, there were several feet of water in her hold and she was settling fast. After something of a struggle, the lifeboat got alongside and took off her crew of seven.

Buddon lifeboat had seen little use for some years and was withdrawn in February 1894 at the request of the Dundee branch committee. Two years earlier, in 1893, St Andrews had been presented with the new lifeboat *Louisa,* the bequest of the late Mrs L.C. Wigney of Twyford. The *Louisa* was launched on the evening of 18 October, 1898, when the schooner *Wilhelm* of Riga went ashore near the mouth of the Eden. One of the *Wilhelm*'s crew had been washed overboard before she struck and five survivors were taken off the wreck. A violent gale, the worst in the 20 years since the loss of the *Merlin,* was still blowing the following day when the Danish brigantine *Kiana* of Marstal was seen trapped in the Bay. Her master was left with no option but to run her ashore on the East Sands. The *Louisa* was being pulled down the narrow cutting in front of the boatshed onto the East Sands when one of the launchers, George Sharp, was run over by the carriage and died soon afterwards. The lifeboat was launched and the crew of the *Kiana* were taken off safely.

Another great storm on Friday, 14 April 1905, drove the *Gesine* of Oldersum, a German schooner inbound with bottles for Alloa Brewery, ashore at Westhaven. The Arbroath lifeboat *James Stevens No.13* was launched shortly before 6.00 a.m. and found the wreck almost submerged with only her forepeak visible among the breakers. The five German crew were so numb with cold that the lifeboat had to lift them off the wreck*.

The gale continued into the following afternoon when the ketch *Diana* of Rye hoisted a distress signal off the pierhead at St Andrews. The *Diana* had arrived at St Andrews with a cargo of gravel two days earlier but had been forced to lie off as the harbour entrance was silted up and too shallow for her to enter. She had ridden out the gale for almost 48 hours until, at 5.00 p.m., her anchor began to drag. The *Louisa* was launched and took off the *Diana*'s crew of eight including the master's wife and child. The *Diana* was brought up within feet of the rocks when her anchor found good holding and was reboarded when the weather moderated two days later.

Apart from one brief period in the 19th century when it received an annual grant from the exchequer, the RNLI has always been entirely dependent on voluntary contributions from members of the public. The finances of the RNLI had reached a paricularly low ebb by the early 1890s and it was realised that two-thirds of its income came from only about 100 people. The fact that whole areas of the country had never been asked to contribute led to the 'Lifeboat Saturday' collections, the first of which to be held in Dundee took place on 24 September 1892. The initial proposal came from the local branch of the Sailors' and Firemens' Union and, essentially a pageant for ordinary people, it was quickly taken up by numerous other bodies and friendly societies in the city.

Mounted on her carriage pulled by eight horses, the *Samuel Shawcross* was drawn eight miles to the village of Lochee. Accompanied by about 400 men on foot and much of the rest of the population of the village in specially laid on tramcars, she then set off to join the main procession gathering at Dundee Esplanade. Waiting for the lifeboat at the Esplanade were 8,000 representatives of the trades of the city including sailors, firemen, brassfounders, masons, carpenters, shipwrights, bakers, mill and factory workers, gardeners, boot and shoemakers, patternmakers, blacksmiths, plasterers, hacklemakers, calender workers,

* Kaiser Wilhelm later presented the Arbroath coxswain, second coxswain and bowman with silver watches inscribed with the Imperial German monogram.

sawmillers, plumbers, brushmakers and the blind workers. Also present were members of Friendly Societies such as the Foresters, the Oddfellows and the Order of Shepherds. There were 13 bands along with contingents from the Boy's Brigade, the training ship *Mars*, Dundee Boating Club, Lochee Swimming Club and David Grant, a survivor of the wreck of the *Forfarshire*.

Part of Dundee's first Lifeboat Saturday parade passing the Albert Institute on 24 September 1892. Pictured is the display mounted by Dundee Boating Club. Poet and tragedian William McGonagall was moved to celebrate the event in verse. The bard had, however, by his own admission, spent the entire afternoon at home reading Lizzie Munro – A Story of Pathos and Peril in the Weekly News, so his impressions were decidedly second-hand. Only fragments of The Life Boat Demonstration have survived;

> *T'was in the year of 1892, and on the 24th September,*
> *Which the inhabitants of Dundee will long remember,*
> *The Great Lifeboat Demonstration*
> *Which caused a great sensation...*
>
> *The Mars boys were there with their band,*
> *Leading the van, which looked very grand.*
>
> *There were a body of sailors all in a row,*
> *And Firemen, Brassfounders, and Operative Masons also,*
> *Besides Carpenters and Joiners and Manchester Oddfellows*
> *And Boilermakers and Blacksmiths that can blow the bellows...*
> *Pattern-makers and Painters most beautiful to be seen*
> *All marching towards the Magdalen Green*
>
> *The bakers, it seems, carried produce:*
> *Such as a big loaf of over fifty pounds,*
> *And the cheers of the spectators had no bounds,*
> *When they saw it held aloft with a sheaf of corn*
> *They declared they never saw the like since they were born.*
> (DUNDEE ART GALLERIES AND MUSEUMS)

Vast crowds lined the route as the cavalcade made its way through the city centre, along the Murraygate, King Street, Princes Street, Victoria Road, Meadowside and into Albert Square. One witness described the scene thus;

The approach of the lifeboat with its gallant crew of belted men was heralded by the cheer which rolled along with its progress, and enthusiastic indeed was the reception which it met with. Coins were showered about the persons of the hardy fishermen who did their best to take on board their heavy catch, and there is no doubt that the 'take' of the lifeboat alone would have been enough to sink her had she been in the water.

'Here they come noo!' was the cry that burst from many throats, and mothers looked anxiously round to see if all their picaninnies were within earshot; fathers mounted their latest-born on their shoulders; little lads and lasses climbed to any available point of vantage; while those who were perched on the Howff walls or ensconced behind windows settled themselves more comfortably. The West Port was a seething mass of humanity and, as far as could be ascertained from a hurried glance, a profitable one for the promoters of the movement.

The afternoon was to have ended with a gathering at Magdalen Green but a sudden rain squall rendered the large flags and banners something of a liability and the parade dispersed from the Hawkhill. A cheque for £847 13s 7d (£847.68), a considerable sum in 1892, was handed over to the RNLI.

The nationwide growth of the Lifeboat Saturday movement was helped considerably by the formation of the first Ladies Auxiliary Committees in 1891. Renamed the Ladies Auxiliary Guilds, they came into their own during the First World War when the Lifeboat Saturday movement collapsed as willing volunteers found more urgent, war-related outlets for their labours. The RNLI was suddenly presented with a cash crisis and the Lifeboat Flag Day was born as a simpler, wartime measure. By 1925, the Dundee Ladies Auxiliary Guild could boast having raised almost £300 out of a total branch income of £380.

St Andrews lifeboat crew taking part in a Lifeboat Saturday parade in Glasgow in June 1896. The nets are being held out to collect coins given by spectators.
(ST ANDREWS PRESERVATION TRUST MUSEUM)

Of the £570 raised by the Dundee Branch in 1932, £485 was raised during the Flag Day held on 18 June which included an entertainment staged in the Victoria Theatre by Dundee Dramatic Society. A further £1 17s 6d was the result of a sale of old golf balls. This fund raising effort continues today with the Ladies Lifeboat Guild contributing £16,000 towards the total branch income for 1994-95 of £66,000. Against this must be set the enormous cost of maintaining and operating modern lifeboats. At 1995 prices, a new D class inshore lifeboat costs around £11,000 and a new offshore lifeboat weighs in at around £1,400,000.

Chapter Seven

THE COMING OF POWER AND THE COMING OF WAR

Wednesday, 26 October 1910 was a cool and rather dull day. The press were giving extensive coverage to the acquittal of Ethel Le Neve on a charge of murder. Her lover, the infamous Dr Hawley Crippen, had been sentenced to death the previous week for killing his wife. The suffragette campaign was at its height and newly deposed King Manuel of Portugal had fled his country straight into the comforting arms of a young English actress. Europe was drifting towards war and mounting concern was being expressed over the parity between the Royal Navy and the German High Seas Fleet. Despite numerous accidents and frequent reports of the dangers of 'aeroplaning', the British Government announced that they would be buying their first two aircraft, Henri Farman biplanes, from France.

Almost exactly 80 years to the day since the first River Tay lifeboat was stationed at Buddon Ness in October 1830, the brand new Broughty Ferry boatshed was colourfully decked out in flags and bunting for the naming of the station's latest lifeboat. The great and good of Broughty society had gathered for the ceremony and 'Griselda', the *Dundee Courier's* society columnist, was there to report on who was who, and what they were wearing.

The naming and dedication ceremony for the Maria *on Wednesday, 26 October 1910.*
(DUNDEE COURIER AND EVENING TELEGRAPH)

59

Lady Ogilvy Dalgliesh, the wife of Dundee Branch President Sir William Ogilvy Dalgleish, recalled being present at the launch of the first *Mary Hartley* in 1862 and handed the new lifeboat over on behalf of her donor, Miss Maria Clark of London. The new boat was then named by the Dundee Branch Captain Superintendent's wife, Mrs Hunter Mitchell; 'I name this boat the *Maria*. God bless all the brave, hardy men who man her.' The *Maria* then shot down the slipway to the accompaniment of loud cheering.

This was not just any naming ceremony; the internal combustion engine had arrived. Experiments with converted pulling and sailing lifeboats had begun in 1905 and the Dundee branch soon realised that a motor lifeboat would free them from having to rely on tugs to tow the lifeboat out to the banks. They first expressed an interest in acquiring one in April 1907. By then, the *Samuel Shawcross,* one of the oldest boats on the Scottish coast, had carried out her last service when, on 3 April 1906, she stood by the disabled Aberdeen steam trawler *Robina.*

The *Maria* was only the fourth purpose-built motor lifeboat constructed for the RNLI. Her 40 horsepower Tylor motor had originally been intended for the new Thurso lifeboat but Thurso had declined the offer, not least because, in such a remote location, nobody had the faintest idea how a petrol engine worked. At 40 feet long and 11 feet in the beam, the 11 ton *Maria* was far too big for the old boatshed. Plans for a larger shed on the site of the existing building had been submitted to Broughty Ferry Burgh Council in July 1908 and triggered a seven month dispute centred on the public toilet and sewer which lay immediately to the east.

The first boatshed had been sited at the bottom of Fort Street in 1862. To rehouse the lifeboat in those days, the carriage was run into the water and a long rope was stretched out of the landward side of the shed and up Fort Street. Hauling on the rope could earn a willing hand a penny and enterprising souls at the front would, on being paid, run round the block to reappear at the tail of the rope before the committee member handing out the coins had reached there.

The Burgh Council were acutely aware of Broughty Ferry's importance both as a tourist resort and as a fashionable suburb of Dundee. Some members were anxious to leave the vista down Fort Street clear of obstructions. The Burgh Police (Scotland) Act of 1892 stated that buildings should not be placed over a sewer and there were those who held the view that a public toilet was more important to the burgh than the lifeboat. The matter was shunted back and forward between the full council and its various committees, despite the fact that these committees were comprised of largely the same small group of people. After four months of wrangling, the council offered an increasingly frustrated RNLI £100 simply to clear the existing site of all buildings and go away - a solution which might have pleased some members of the council but would have left the lifeboat homeless.

Pressure must have been brought to bear as, in February 1909, the council suddenly relented and allowed construction work on the original site on the condition that the new building extend no closer to the sewer than the previous boatshed. The completed boatshed cost £1,700 and still stands slightly off-centre of Fort Street. None of the houses in the old part of the village had electricity and the Burgh Council agreed, albeit reluctantly, to bring a special supply from King Street on the condition that the RNLI provide an annual guarantee of £6. Construction work had been completed by the time the *Maria* arrived at Broughty Ferry on Tuesday, 11 October 1910*.

The new lifeboat and boatshed at Broughty Ferry were not the only changes during this eventful period. Coxswain John Lorimer retired after 23 years of lifeboat service and was succeeded by David Webster. George Peebles was appointed the station's first full time motor mechanic. James Hunter jun., honorary secretary since taking over from James MacEwen in

---

* Along with its peculiar brand of parish-pump politics, Broughty Ferry Burgh Council was consigned to history when the burgh was absorbed by Dundee in 1913. The public toilet has disappeared but the sewer, better known to today's lifeboat crews as the 'poo-pipe', remains an ever-present, unsavoury hazard, particularly during low tide launches.

1864, died and a fellow lawyer, David Dempster, was elected in his place. Another naming ceremony took place in St Andrews less than two weeks after that for the *Maria*. Here too, a new boatshed had been built at the East Bents and a large gathering witnessed the naming of the new 35 foot pulling and sailing self-righter *John and Sarah Hatfield*.

From the Broughty Ferry Guide and Carnoustie Gazette *for Friday, 14 October 1910;*

ARRIVAL OF THE MOTOR LIFEBOAT

The new motor lifeboat arrived at Broughty Ferry on Tuesday, and was safely housed to await the launching ceremony. Leaving Harwich on Friday morning, she called for exhibition purposes at various ports en route. making a stay at Scarborough, the Tyne and Berwick, and leaving the last named place on Monday. When the boat, which is named the Maria, *came opposite the lifeboat shed, a large crowd gathered in the vicinity, remaining until the work of housing was complete. She is 40 by 11 feet, is of the Watson design, weighs 11 tons, is fitted with a Tylor motor and has a speed of seven knots an hour. She is, like the lifeboat shed itself, very well equipped, and cost a good round sum.*

(THE ROYAL NATIONAL LIFEBOAT INSITUTION)

The *Maria* was launched just after 9.00 a.m. on Saturday, 18 March 1911 after a vessel was reported in a dangerous position south of the Abertay Sands. Coxswain Webster took the lifeboat through The Pool in an easterly gale and sleet showers, shipping a number of seas on the way, and found the Stavanger registered schooner *Oloa Pauline* trapped behind the banks. Her master seemed unaware of his perilous position and, clearly thinking he was in the Forth, told David Webster that he wanted to continue on his way to Granton. Webster had to persuade the reluctant Norwegian to follow him back through The Pool into deep water and on to anchor at Broughty Ferry. On this, her first service, the *Maria* gave great satisfaction in very bad weather.

On the evening of 3 November 1911, David Webster received a telephone message that a large steamer was ashore on the Gaa Sands and burning distress flares. The *Maria* was launched into a south-westerly gale and reached the SS *Claus Horn* of Lubeck, inbound from Archangel with 4,000 tons of timber at 9.50 p.m. Waves swept the steamer's decks and, from messages shouted over the roaring of the sea, it became apparent that she had run short of bunker coal. The *Maria* stood by until 2.00 a.m. when, using the sweepings from her bunkers, the *Claus Horn* struggled off the banks and up river to anchor off Broughty Ferry.

The fishing smack *Resolute* of Leith anchored off Kinkell Braes, east of St Andrews, as an easterly gale blew up on Saturday, 21 September 1912. Eight days later, the storm still raged and the *Resolute* was still at anchor. A close watch was being kept on her and, just after 2.00 p.m., her anchor cable was seen to part. The *John and Sarah Hatfield* was launched and took off her three crew, exhausted after their long ordeal, just minutes before the fishing boat struck rocks and sank.

The storm was still raging two days later, on Monday, 30 September, when the 366 ton barque *Prinses Wilhelmina* arrived with a cargo of timber at the Tay fairway buoy after a wild passage from the Gulf of Finland. There was no sign of the pilot cutter and Captain Johnsson decided not to attempt the Tay on his own in bad weather. Turning his ship around to make for shelter in the Forth, he was unable to weather the Carr Rocks off Fife Ness and put back to lie to two anchors in St Andrews Bay.

The storm grew even more intense as the night wore on and the wind backed to the northeast. One of the anchor cables snapped and ropes were taken round the mainmast and deckhouse to relieve the strain on the the windlass holding the second cable. The remaining anchor could not hold the *Prinses Wilhelmina* and soon began to drag. Johnsson first tried to run her ashore on the West Sands but, when still about a mile off, her steering was smashed beyond repair and she drifted onto rocks below St Andrews Castle.

The St Andrews lifeboat John and Sarah Hatfield *approaching the wreck of the* Prinses Wilhelmina *below St Andrews Castle on Saturday, 1 October 1912. St Andrews Rocket Bridgade fired three lines across the wreck but, just then, the lifeboat got free of the surf and, as seen here, pulled under her starboard side.*
(ST ANDREWS PRESERVATION TRUST MUSEUM)

Watched by a large crowd, Coxswain Jamie Chisholm brings the John and Sarah Hatfield *round the pierhead at St Andrews with the nine survivors from the* Prinses Wilhelmina.
(ST ANDREWS PRESERVATION TRUST MUSEUM)

Men and women waded up to their necks in the surf to launch the *John and Sarah Hatfield* and Coxswain Chisholm got all nine of the *Prinses Wilhelmina*'s crew aboard the lifeboat and safely into the harbour. The ship's cat had to be left but was found safe and well the following day when the wreck was boarded at low tide. James Chisholm was awarded the RNLI's silver medal for gallantry and a grateful Captain Johnsson presented him with two handsome chairs which had graced his cabin*.

An early sign of the military build-up that preceded the outbreak of the First World War came in July 1909 when the Admiralty yacht *Enchantress* arrived to inspect naval facilities being developed in Dundee Harbour. On board were Admiral Sir John Jellicoe, later to command the Grand Fleet at the Battle of Jutland, First Sea Lord Admiral 'Jacky' Fisher and Dundee's ambitious young MP, Winston Churchill. The Admiralty signed an agreement with the Harbour Trustees which gave the Royal Navy the exclusive use of the West Graving Dock and part of King William IV Dock. A coaling depot for destroyers and torpedo boats was sited next to the entrance to Camperdown Dock. HMS *Vulcan*, the depot ship of the 7th Submarine Flotilla, arrived that November with her squadron of 'C' class submarines and destroyers.

St Andrews lifeboat station closed in 1938 but, as can be seen in this photograph taken at the same spot 82 years after the Prinses Wilhelmina *service, the lifesaving continues. The Broughty Ferry inshore and offshore lifeboats were launched on service on 43 occasions during 1995.*

Helmsman Bob Jeffrey brings the Broughty Ferry inshore lifeboat Captain Colin *into St Andrews Harbour on the afternoon of Sunday, 28 August 1994. The ILB had been launched after horrified onlookers at Kinshaldy beach reported that two girls on an inflatable raft were being swept out to sea by a stiff offshore breeze. The ILB crew reached the scene within 15 minutes to find one of the teenagers suffering from hypothermia. Both were landed safely and made a full recovery.*

The sea temperature around the east coast of Scotland rarely rises above ten degrees and, survival time in the winter, when it can drop well below freezing point, may be measured in minutes. Even in high summer, hypothermia can kill the ill-equipped and unfit in well under an hour.

(MURRAY BROWN)

---

* One of these chairs is among a number of relics from the *Princess Wilhelmina* displayed in the St Andrews Preservation Trust museum.

The *Maria* was launched to stand by a Goole registered schooner, the *Dalmaris,* which was in danger close to the banks on 8 February, 1914. The following morning, a small seaplane took off from North Queensferry crewed by Major Gordon and Leading Seaman Shaw of what was then the Naval Wing of the Royal Flying Corps. They turned north and, after 56 minutes flying time, touched down on the the Tay and taxied in to the new flying boat base at RFC Stannergate. The seaplane tender HMS *Hermes* had visited the Tay to test flying conditions in 1912 and, in 1913, the Admiralty had leased a large area of ground at Carolina Port. Much infilling had to be carried out to provide stable ground on which to build hangars and slipways and a large accommodation site was constructed between what is now Craigie Drive and the railway at Stannergate Station.

Coxswain David Webster (right) and the crew of the Broughty Ferry lifeboat Maria *before the First World War. Standing second from left is Charles Gall, a former fisherman and boatswain with the Brocklebank line, who joined the lifeboat crew in 1910. Gall took over as coxswain in 1915 and, in 1922, was awarded an RNLI silver medal for the rescue of the crew of the pilot cutter* Daydream. *As coxswain of the* John Ryburn, *he was badly injured during a service in November 1927 and retired from the lifeboat service three years later. He died in September 1937.*
(DUNDEE ART GALLERIES AND MUSEUMS)

The outbreak of war in 1914 was just weeks away when the Imperial German Navy cruiser *Augsburg* visited the Tay. For the last time, German and British sailors were seen arm-in-arm on Dundee's streets as they sampled the dubious delights of the city's pubs. The first invasion scare took place on 8 August, just four days after war was declared, when an unlit trawler entered the river. A large force of territorials was deployed around Broughty Ferry.

St Andrews lifeboat, the *John and Sarah Hatfield* gave assistance when the Norwegian barque *Salem* was wrecked on Kinshaldy Beach on 3 November 1914 and, on 13 December, she stood by when the Danish steamer *Helene* went ashore near the mouth of the Eden after her anchor cables parted in a south-easterly gale. The *Maria* was also launched from Broughty Ferry but, on this occasion, her engine refused to start.

Efforts to refloat the *Helene* were beginning at 9.00 a.m. on 15 December when St Andrews coastguard telephoned Coxswain Webster at Broughty Ferry with the news that a seaplane had been seen landing next to the Abertay Sands and firing distress rockets. The *Maria* was launched at 9.07 a.m. and earned for herself the distinction of being the first lifeboat to be called out to an aircraft in distress. She stood by as a trawler picked up Lt Stewart and Mechanic Johnstone and towed the Short seaplane back to the Stannergate base.

A vicious south-easterly storm was raging twelve days later on Sunday, 27 December. At around 4.00 a.m., HMS *Success*, one of a flotilla of destroyers steaming south to the new naval base at Rosyth, lost her course in the wartime blackout and ran ashore at Cambo Briggs, two miles west of Fife Ness. She sent an SOS which brought two other destroyers and two minesweepers to her assistance but they were unable to get close. Coxswain Andrew Cunningham of the Crail lifeboat *Edwin Kay* was alerted by the coastguard at about 6.00 a.m. He immediately roused his crew, though he had to call at their houses individually as the firing of the maroons was banned under wartime restrictions. The Crail men made their way to the boatshed at Balcomie, launched their boat, and covered the three miles to Cambo by 8.00 a.m. One of the lifeboatmen described the scene as Cunningham took *Edwin Kay* under the leeward side of the destroyer;

> We found the destroyer in a pitiful plight. She was a four-funnelled vessel and two of the funnels were under water when we reached her. All of the crew were wearing lifebelts, and most of them had dispensed with the greater part of their clothing - those of them that had it on when the accident occurred. They were clinging to the funnels and rails round that part of the stern that was still above the water.

HMS Success *in happier days (above) and (below) on Cambo Briggs.*
(CRAIL MUSEUM)

The *Edwin Kay* landed her first 17 men, the youngest of the destroyer's crew, at Kingsbarns, then set out again for the wreck. Just as she was leaving the shore, a particularly large wave carried the lifeboat onto an old beacon, the centre spike of which tore two gashes in her hull, one of them almost three feet long. Another wave swept Andrew Cunningham and crewman Charlie Dewar overboard. Both were recovered safely but not before Coxswain Cunningham came desperately close to being crushed between the lifeboat and the framework of the beacon. Despite her damage, the *Edwin Kay* made two more trips out to the stranded destroyer to bring off another 40 men. As she completed her third trip, the Crail men saw the St Andrews lifeboat bearing down on the destroyer and beached their battered craft.

St Andrews coxswain Jamie Chisholm had caused something of a stir when, at 7.00 a.m. and in flagrant violation of the wartime regulations, he fired the maroons.* Chisholm said later;

When we approached the scene of the wreck, we could not see the ship owing to a blinding hailstorm. When this passed off, we could see two masts and a portion of the stern. We moved forward until within 400 yards of the destroyer, and saw the Crail lifeboat coming from the beach. Our position was a dangerous one and I realised that the quickest and best means of reaching the vessel was to go over the Cambo Briggs rocks. We had no time to think of anything else and I trusted to the high seas rushing us over the rocks and into safe quarters.

We then got close to the wreck, and by that time the Crail boat had been so damaged as to be rendered useless. There were 13 men on board the *Success* including the Captain and four officers, and I saw them clinging to the stern. We called to the men to leap onto the lifeboat, but they replied, 'We cannot leave until we get orders from our Captain.' I could not see the Captain - in fact I could not tell an officer from an ordinary seaman. Their clothing was all tattered and torn, and afterwards I learned the Captain was the man whom I had first seen standing naked.

The first Crail lifeboat, the George Paterson, *went on station on 6 November 1884 but saw little use. Her replacement in January 1910, the* Edwin Kay, *seen here being launched at Balcomie, saved 84 lives including 54 from HMS* Success. *Crail lifeboat station closed on 31 March 1923 though the boatshed survives as a greenkeeper's hut for the Balcomie golf course.*
(CRAIL MUSEUM)

Lieutenant Pennefather, the destroyer's commander, left the St Andrews crew in a position of considerable danger for fully 45 minutes while he made up his mind what to do. Eventually, Chisholm's patience with the man ran out and he told him in the strongest possible terms that either he ordered his men into the lifeboat, or Chisholm would assume that his services were

---

* Scarborough, Whitby and Hartlepool had been shelled by German warships on the morning of 16 December and many startled St Andreans thought the exploding maroons were the opening rounds of an enemy naval barrage. The townspeople were already jittery thanks to the ineffable Earl of Crawford and Balcarres who had informed a bemused House of Lords that Fife was 'overrun with enemy agents' and that, every night, they were signalling vital information to U boats lying off the coast!

no longer required and would see to the safety of his own crew. At that, Pennefather and the remaining men wasted no time in getting into the lifeboat and were taken to St Andrews to be looked after in the Grand Hotel.

At Kingsbarns, meanwhile, the rest of the survivors gave three hearty cheers for Andrew Cunningham and the Crail crew. Singing *It's a long way to Tipperaray,* they marched up the track from the beach to the Kingsbarns School where the Crail and Kingsbarns villagers had prepared hot drinks and dry clothing. One sailor turned to his friend who was wearing a decidedly 'horsey' jacket and said, 'Yew'll be awlrait fer the hinds then, Mate!'

The extraordinary endeavours of Coxswain Cunningham and his crew won nationwide admiration. Among many plaudits and rewards were an RNLI silver medal for Cunningham and a cheque for £7 to be divided among the crew from the officer's mess of the Cape Light Horse Regiment in South Africa.

Four days after the wreck of the *Success,* on New Year's morning, a seaplane took off from the Stannergate base to search for a U boat that had been reported off Fife Ness. A strong easterly wind was still blowing and, by 8.00 a.m., the aircraft had only reached Kingsbarns where it was forced down within sight of the wrecked

Coxswain Andrew Cunningham completed 35 years in the lifeboat service before retiring in October 1919. He is wearing the silver medal awarded for the service to HMS Success.
(CRAIL MUSEUM)

destroyer. Fishermen Robert Brown, Archie Ritchie and his brother David launched a small partan yawl, the *Barbara,* and picked up the two frozen airmen after they had been in the water for over an hour.

Unable to return to Kingsbarns due to the weather, Brown set a course for St Andrews. They had only gone two miles when they were met by the *John and Sarah Hatfield* and Coxswain Chisholm suggested they all transfer into the lifeboat. The yawl was plunging and rolling in heavy seas and the terrified, seasick airmen showed a marked reluctance to attempt a transfer to another boat. The *Barbara* carried on into St Andrews and, despite being almost swamped by a huge wave which threw her against the pierhead, reached harbour safely. The airmen were taken to the Marine Hotel to recover and Robert Brown was awarded the RNLI's silver medal.

Broughty Ferry, Arbroath and St Andrews lifeboats were all launched into a southerly gale on the morning of 25 October 1915 after the 10,500 ton cruiser HMS *Argyll* ran full tilt onto the blacked out Bell Rock just yards from the lighthouse and the spot where the *Quixotic* would founder 24 years later. The cruiser had a crew of 655, far in excess of the number the three lifeboats could possibly carry. Thanks to some superb shiphandling, the destroyers *Hornet* and *Jackal* were able to get alongside the cruiser to take off her crew and the lifeboats were not required. To this day, the rusting remains of both HMS *Success* and HMS *Argyll* lie where they went ashore, the much-frequented haunts of amateur divers.

The inadequate Tay pilotage service had been blamed for the loss of the *Prinses Wilhelmina* in 1912. The problems persisted, largely due to the lack of steam cutters, but competition, primarily with Leith, was fierce and the extra cost of running steam vessels was felt to be prohibitive. During the war years, the pilots, not unreasonably, objected to acting as sitting targets for any Zeppelin or U boat that happened to be passing and the Admiralty, who controlled the port, provided them with a steam drifter, the *Mary Adoline*. Accidental casualties at the river entrance were dramatically reduced as a result.

The largest wartime casualty had been the jute liner *Clan Shaw* which, in January 1917, hit a mine laid close to the fairway buoy by a U boat.* The wreck of the *Clan Shaw* lay right in the centre of the navigable channel and was a considerable hazard to navigation. The harbour trustees took the view that the wreck was the result of an act of war and that it was the responsibility of the Admiralty to remove it, or reduce it until it presented no hazard to navigation.

James Chisholm was appointed coxswain of the St Andrews Lifeboat in 1892. He won an RNLI silver medal for the rescue of the crew of the Prinses Wilhelmina *in 1912 and took part in the service to the destroyer* Success *in 1914. He is wearing the cumbersome cork lifejacket issued to 19th century lifeboatmen.*

(ST ANDREWS PRESERVATION TRUST MUSEUM)

Meanwhile, rather than spend money on proper wreck marker buoys, the trustees elected to mark the *Clan Shaw* with the old fairway buoy. This extraordinary decision was bound to lead to disaster and, sure enough, four ships struck the wreck during 1919. The Harbour Trust were left contemplating utter ruin as damages claims amounting to the then astronomical sum of £600,000 were raised against them. Litigation lasted three years before the trustees were forced to pay out well over £100,000 in addition to the £6,000 they had to stump up for the removal of the wreck.

The steam cutter was withdrawn when the Admiralty relinquished control of the port at the end of the war and two old sailing cutters were pressed back into service. The *Tay* had been built in Dundee in 1862 and the *Daydream* was originally a racing yawl built at Cowes in 1871. Converted to a cruising yacht, she had been purchased for use as a pilot cutter in 1894. Both were in poor condition by 1919 and leaked badly in heavy weather. When one of the ships struck the *Clan Shaw* wreck, pilots were to be seen chasing after her in a rowing boat, this being a somewhat faster mode of travel than the cutter herself!

The difficulties surrounding the pilotage service came to a head late on Saturday 10 April 1920 when the old *Daydream* missed stays off Buddon Ness and fell onto the Gaa Sands on a strong ebb tide. As soon as she began bumping heavily on the sandbank, it was clear to Captain Macdonald Cameron that the cutter was doomed. Distress rockets were fired just before midnight and, at 1.20 a.m., Pilot William Watson climbed the wildly swaying mast with a signal lamp and flashed morse distress signals to Carnoustie coastguard station. Back came the reassuring message, 'Sending lifeboat'.

The *Maria* had been launched at 1.05 a.m. and reached the Gaa Sands at 2.00 a.m. By then, the *Daydream* was making water fast and starting to break up. Her oil-fired stove had overturned and started a fire down below. Coxswain Charles Gall made several attempts to get alongside the rolling cutter but each time the rowing boat hanging in her davits threatened to come crashing down on top of the lifeboat. Gall shouted to the crew of the cutter to cut the boat away but Captain Cameron misunderstood, thinking that Gall wanted the pilots to use it

---

* The *UC41* (Leutnant Foerste) was depth charged and sunk near the Tay fairway buoy by the minesweeper HMS *Jacinth* (Lt. Cdr. Gray DSO RNR) after being caught laying mines on the evening of 21 August 1917.

to transfer to the lifeboat. The boat was swept out of sight by a large wave after the tackles snapped when Pilot William Ferrier jumped aboard.

Five times Charles Gall brought the *Maria* alongside the cutter. Four pilots jumped to safety on the second attempt, Captain Cameron making it across on the fifth attempt as the lifeboat came desperately close to being driven right over the wreck. The *Maria* then went in search of William Ferrier and found him in the waterlogged rowing boat, bailing for all he was worth and lighting matches in an attempt to attract attention. He was so cold and exhausted that two lifeboatmen had to climb down and lift him aboard the *Maria*.

An undated photograph of RNLB Maria *under way off West Ferry.* Maria *was only the fourth motor lifeboat constructed for the RNLI and, despite being underpowered by today's standards, she represented a huge leap forward in lifeboat technology.*
(THE ROYAL NATIONAL LIFEBOAT INSITUTION)

Coxswain Gall was awarded a richly-deserved bronze medal by the RNLI for this service which was destined to be almost the last for the *Maria*. On 13 May that year she rescued Tayport fisherman Henry Harley from his mussel boat *The Joyce* which was sinking near the Horseshoe Buoy. The former Peterhead lifeboat, the *John Ryburn,* was placed on station at Broughty Ferry in 1921 and, after an illustrious career in which she saved 14 lives, the old pioneer motor lifeboat *Maria* eventually became the yacht *Passerelle*. Sadly, she was wrecked during a storm in 1991 and subsequently burned.

The loss of the *Daydream* and the hugely expensive litigation surrounding the *Clan Shaw* finally forced the harbour trustees to take action. Pilotage was made compulsory and the former Great Yarmouth steam drifter *Captain Fryatt* was purchased as a replacement cutter.

Chapter Eight

To the Service of Humanity

In marked contrast to her service life at Peterhead where she saved 158 lives, the *John Ryburn* was to have a relatively uneventful career at Broughty Ferry. On 26 January 1922 she stood by the Belgian steamer *Rosa* and, the following day, she was launched when the galliot *Hayo*, Tyne bound from Norway with pit props, went ashore at Westhaven. The *Hayo's* crew were saved by the Arbroath Rocket Brigade and the lifeboat's services were not required. A ferry still ran between Broughty Ferry and Tayport in 1922 and, on 8 April, the *John Ryburn* towed in the disabled ferryboat *Abertay* with her four passengers and two crew. The inbound Ellerman jute liner *City of Manchester* went aground on the Abertay Sands at 2.45 a.m. on 10 February 1924. The *John Ryburn* stood by until she floated off on the tide at 6.00 a.m.

Dundee's first BBC wireless service, Station 2DE, began broadcasting from studios in Lochee Road in November 1924. At 10.30 p.m. on 22 December 1924, the SS *Chingford* sailed from Dundee bound for Grangemouth and the Tyne with a part cargo of timber. Captain Chapman took his ship, which was owned by Dundee RNLI Branch President and shipping magnate James Hunter Mitchell, safely round the North Carr lightship. At about 2.30 a.m., however, in poor visibility and a westerly gale, he ran her ashore in Goat's Bay, a mile east of Crail.

The pulling and sailing Anstruther lifeboat *James and Mary Walker,* Broughty Ferry and St Andrews lifeboats all launched though the latter two had a considerable distance to cover in dreadful weather to reach the wrecked steamer. Coxswain Martin Gardner and the crew of the *James and Mary Walker* were first to reach the *Chingford*. They found the Crail Rocket Brigade had already put a line aboard the wreck and had taken six men off. With some difficulty due to the waves crashing against the wrecked steamer's port side, the remaining 12 crewmen from the *Chingford* were taken aboard the Anstruther lifeboat and neither the Broughty Ferry nor the St Andrews boat's services were required.

Broughty Ferry lifeboatmen performed an unusual service, right on their own doorstep, on Wednesday, 26 January 1927. The Rix Line coaster *Robrix* had left Perth that morning bound for Hull but encountered a south-easterly gale and heavy seas on The Bar. She turned back but suffered engine failure on her way up river and, after narrowly missing the Ferry Rock, drifted ashore at Broughty Ferry between the lifeboat shed and the Pilot Pier. Bowman John Stewart waded out to take a line from the coaster but this parted as she lay over to starboard on the ebbing tide. Helped by Motor Mechanic Matt Standing and Second Mechanic John Gall, he secured the ship using a wire rope. The *Robrix* ended up just 20 feet from Fisher Street but was refloated the following day.

The *John Ryburn* was launched into a violent storm at 12.30 p.m. on Tuesday, 22 November 1927, when the Estonian barque *Uku*, Dundee bound with firewood, went ashore on the Gaa Sands. The lifeboat battled down river, passing four large steamers that had been forced to turn back by the huge seas crashing across The Bar. As she closed the wreck of the *Uku*, a massive sea struck her, tearing the wheel from Coxswain Charles Gall's hands. Second Coxswain Alex Gall recalled the moment when one of the whirling spokes struck his brother in the face;

> The seas were running very high, far higher than I have ever seen them, and when we were not far from the edge of the bank, an unusually heavy sea swept over our starboard bow, swamping us. Although I was clinging to two ropes, I was knocked up against the coxswain and saw his face all covered with blood. Another sea filled us completely and, although the engine was put on full speed, she would neither go back nor forward. She got fair mesmerised and if another sea had been shipped we would not have had any chance, but fortunately she recovered splendidly and righted. We wanted to go back with the coxswain but he would not hear tell of it.

Despite Charles Gall's protests, his brother did take the wheel and made for the pilot cutter lying at anchor in the partial lee of Buddon Ness. Matt Standing said later that, when the *John Ryburn* shipped the waves, she filled until all he could see was the top of the mast sticking out of the water and it was only when the sea began to drain out that he knew he was still aboard. He continued;

When we drew alongside the pilot cutter, we shouted to them to throw down some first aid equipment for the coxswain, and one of the pilots wrapped some articles in his cap and threw them over the side. As he did so, a huge wave lifted us into the air and, for a moment, the cutter and the lifeboat were riding the tops of neighbouring waves and we were in imminent danger of fouling her anchor. The coxswain, despite his injury, retained his presence of mind and shouted to me, "Open her full out, Matt" I did so. We were alongside the cutter at that moment, and we simply cut through everything. Then the mast snapped in two and fell among us. It struck me on the shoulder, making it black and blue.

Once Charles Gall had been given first aid, the lifeboat returned to the Gaa Sands and again attempted, unsuccessfully, to close the wreck of the *Uku*. Meanwhile, thousands of sightseers had gathered to watch as, except for the mate who was drowned, the crew of the *Uku* were dragged ashore by the Rocket Brigades from Arbroath and Carnoustie. The wreck was known to local children as the *Yookiyoo* and her remains sticking out of the sand became a tourist attraction.

The *John Ryburn* stood by on 26 April 1930 as the *James and Mary Walker* tried to rescue the crew of the Aberdeen trawler *George Aunger* which had run ashore on the Isle of May in the entrance to the River Forth. In the event, one of the Isle of May lightkeepers climbed aboard the trawler and saved four of her crew but not before the skipper and a fireman had been washed overboard. Another Aberdeen steam trawler, the *Loch Long,* sailed from Aberdeen at 6.30 p.m. on Sunday, 8 March 1931, bound for the coaling berth at Leith. Skipper Charles Chisholm stayed in the wheelhouse until the North Carr lightship was sighted at 1.00 a.m. then went to his bunk leaving the mate, John Allan, in charge. Forty minutes later, in a blinding snowstorm and northerly gale, she crashed onto Balcomie Briggs at Fife Ness.

The Aberdeen steam trawler Loch Long *went ashore on Balcomie Briggs near Fife Ness in the early hours of Monday, 9 March 1931. Broughty Ferry, St Andrews and Anstruther lifeboats were launched in response to her distress flares and, in a particularly hazardous rescue carried out in a blizzard, the St Andrews lifeboat took off her crew of ten. Originally built for the Admiralty in 1917 as the Castle Class trawler* Timothy Crawley, *she became the* Loch Long *on being sold to the Loch Line Steam Trawling and Fishing Company of Abrdeen service in the Second World War. Returning once more to the fishing in 1947, she was finally broken up in 1956.*
(DUNDEE COURIER AND EVENING TELEGRAPH)

Her distress rockets were seen by coastguards at Fife Ness and the St Andrews, Anstruther and Broughty Ferry lifeboats were all launched. The maroons were fired over St Andrews at 2.10 a.m. but Coxswain David Fenton found himself short of two crew for the *John and Sarah Hatfield*. From the crowd of 200 that gathered at the East Bents to help launch the boat, Bob Henrit, a golf professional, and Bob Duncan, the starter on the Eden Course, volunteered their services. The lifeboat was launched into the surf at 2.30 a.m. and rowed for about a mile into clear water before sail was hoisted.

The former Buckie drifter Titania *beached among the breakers off the entrance to St Andrews Harbour on 9 March 1931. The St Andrews lifeboat* John and Sarah Hatfield *was launched for the second time on that bitterly cold Monday and saved the drifter's crew of five.*
(DUNDEE COURIER AND EVENING TELEGRAPH)

The crew of the *Loch Long* were relieved to see all three lifeboats bearing down on them at the same time. The St Andrews boat arrived first and Coxswain Fenton dropped anchor then veered down onto the stranded trawler, bumping over a submerged rock on the way. As the Anstruther and Broughty Ferry boats stood by, all ten of the trawler's crew were taken aboard the *John and Sarah Hatfield*. David Fenton and his crew brought the lifeboat back to St Andrews at 8.30 a.m. and the trawlermen were looked after at the Cross Keys Hotel.

The *John and Sarah Hatfield* was still lying afloat in St Andrews Harbour when the maroons were fired again early that afternoon. The Buckie drifter *Titania* had left Tayport that morning bound for the west coast via the Forth and Clyde Canal. She was only a mile out from the fairway buoy when she sprang a serious leak. Her pumps were unable to keep up with the intake and Skipper Jim Campbell decided to make for St Andrews. She was just off the harbour mouth when the water reached her fires and she lost all power and quickly sank. The *John and Sarah Hatfield* was hurriedly manned again and saved the *Titania*'s crew of five. The wreck of the *Titania* was driven up the East Sands on the next flood tide but the *Loch Long* was later pulled off Balcomie Rocks by the salvage steamer *Henry Lancaster*.

David Fenton received a message that another trawler, the *Spes Bona* of Eyemouth, was aground on the Carr Rocks at 10.30 p.m. on Wednesday, 9 March 1932. Excitement got the better of the crowd attracted to the East Bents by the firing of the maroons and over-willing helpers started pulling the boat down the slipway towards the East Sands. As the carriage swerved out of control up the grassy bank in front of the boatshed, Pat Flannigan tripped over the rope he was pulling and fell under one of the carriage wheels.

The *John and Sarah Hatfield* was launched but reached the Carr Rock only to find that the *Spes Bona* had refloated on the tide and was nowhere to be seen. Pat Flannigan died in St Andrews Cottage Hospital and was buried in the Western Cemetery three days later. Led by Coxswain Fenton, the lifeboat crew walked on either side of the hearse and Flannigan's widow was granted an RNLI pension.

Broughty Ferry lifeboat was launched on the night of 15 April 1933 to stand by the trawler *Dulcibelle* which was in difficulties in a south-westerly gale. On 17 January 1934, in full view of passengers in a train crossing the Tay Bridge, the sandboat *Inchmor* capsized in a westerly gale and sank off Newport Pier. The Tay sandboats were generally old, leaky and unsafe. The *Inchmor* was no exception, having been built to carry water and horses during the Crimean War. The *John Ryburn*, the steam lighter *Charles Barrie*, the LNER tender Inchcape and the Tay Ferry *B.L. Nairn* all went to the rescue but only Skipper James Law of Dundee was picked up by the *B.L. Nairn*.

Members of the John Ryburn's *crew pictured towards the end of her career in 1935. At left, newly appointed Motor Mechanic Johnny Grieve. On his left, at rear, are Coxswain Alex Gall, Bowman Jimmy Gall and Coxswain Jim Lorimer.*
(VINA ROBERTSON)

By 1934, the *John Ryburn* was 19 years old and nearing the end of her service life. Coxswain Alex Gall and Second Coxswain James Lorimer were also both due to retire. On 14 January, three days before the *Inchmor* service, the branch committee met to consider Gall and Lorimer's impending retiral and the arrangements for a new lifeboat due in 1935. It was proving impossible to find the right man for the position of coxswain on a retainer fee so, for the first time, it was decided that a full-time coxswain should be appointed.

Coxswain David Fenton and the crew of the St Andrews lifeboat in 1934. The boatshed built in 1910 to house the John and Sarah Hatfield *survives today as the home of St Andrews Sailing Club. Two previous lifeboat sheds have occupied the East Bents site; the first boatshed was built here in 1802 to house Henry Greathead's Cork Lifeboat. The 1860 boatshed built for the* Annie *also occupied this site.*
(ST ANDREWS UNIVERSITY LIBRARY PHOTOGRAPHIC COLLECTION)

The vacancy was advertised in the autumn of 1934 at a weekly wage of £3. This caused the first of a series of embarrassments when somebody realised that the motor mechanic was already being paid £3. 10/- (£3.50) per week. From 17 applicants, three from Broughty Ferry and one from Montrose were selected for interview. One of the Broughty men withdrew on getting another job and another was not suitable as he had no lifeboat experience. The remaining Broughty man was offered the job but failed the medical as he was colour-blind. Montrose fisherman Jim Coull, bowman of the Montrose lifeboat, was then offered the job.

News of Jim Coull's appointment generated a storm of protest. It was the view in Broughty Ferry that there was no need to break with decades of tradition by going elsewhere for a coxswain. Well-attended protest meetings in St James' Hall resulted in a 170 signature petition, though this was rejected by the branch committee. An unholy row blew up with crew threatening to boycott the boat and subscribers threatening to withdraw their support. Local councillor James Gillies wrote a strongly worded letter of protest to the RNLI who replied that the appointment of a coxswain was a purely local matter. Gillies did calm some of the inflamed passions and stressed that the lifeboat must always be manned.

The harsh reality was that the days of local fishermen forming the lifeboat crew were numbered. The Broughty Ferry fishing fleet had peaked in 1880s with upwards of 80 boats and 180 fishermen. The advent of steam trawlers based at Dundee, Granton, Anstruther and Arbroath along with subsequent over-fishing meant that, by 1900, there were just 50 boats. Much of the Scottish herring catch had been exported to Russia and Germany until war in 1914 and revolution in 1916 closed these markets down overnight. Broughty Ferry fishing boats were old, small and out of date so that when a shoal of big, full fish appeared in the Tay in the winter of 1936, Granton and Arbroath trawlers were able to clean it up. There would be only four boats and six full-time fishermen left by 1948.

Coxswain David Fenton takes the St Andrews lifeboat out on exercise in the mid 1930s. By then, the John and Sarah Hatfield *was 26 years old and one of the last pulling and sailing boats on the Scottish coast. Launching into the sheltered waters of the inner harbour, as illustrated here, was only possible at high tide and St Andrews was felt to be unsuitable for all-tide, all-weather motor lifeboat operations.*
(ST ANDREWS UNIVERSITY LIBRARY PHOTOGRAPHIC COLLECTION)

As the fishing industry declined, many of the former fishermen and their families found work in Dundee's textile mills or the Caledon shipyard until the great depression of the early 1930s threw many of them back out of work. In stark contrast to the opulence of neighbouring West Ferry where the jute barons and merchant princes had their palatial mansions, housing in the old village was poor, overcrowded and insanitary. Outbreaks of scarlet fever, influenza, whooping cough, measles and tuberculosis found rich pickings in such surroundings. Infant mortality was on the increase. Against such a poverty-stricken background, it is hardly surprising that many felt that a new wage coming into the village should go to a Broughty family.

Jim Coull's appointment went ahead despite the protests. Bowman Jimmy 'Painter' Gall was made second coxswain and George Smith was promoted from signalman to bowman. Coull handled a difficult situation well and with dignity. One of his first actions was to ask local fishermen to show him the hidden banks and channels of the Tay estuary.

Coxswain Coull accepted the new lifeboat *Mona* from the yard of Groves and Guttridge on the Isle of Wight and sailed north from Cowes on Thursday, 2 May 1935, in company with the new Barnett class lifeboat *Rankin* bound for Aith in the Shetland Islands. The two boats sailed into Broughty Ferry four days later and the *John Ryburn* eventually became the yacht *Bembo* which was still afloat on the Welsh coast in 1996.

Malcolm Campbell had taken the world land speed record to 301 mph in *Bluebird* and the streamlined LNER locomotive Silver Bullet had just set a new British rail speed record of 112 mph. British golfers were being roundly beaten in the Ryder Cup, the Cunard liner *Queen Mary* was fitting out at Clydebank, Dundee's Mills Observatory had just opened and fascist speakers were being beaten up at public meetings in the city's Westport. It was Saturday, 28 September 1935, and, in pursuit of his ambitions for a latter-day Roman empire, Mussolini was busy provoking a war in Abyssinia. That afternoon, in a rainstorm, the *Mona* was christened at King George V Wharf.

Rising and falling on the misty river, her paintwork gleaming, the *Mona* was dwarfed by the great cargo liners around her. The VIP platform had been moved into the rather bleak surroundings of a transit shed and the service opened with that great hymn of the sea, *Eternal Father, strong to save*. The D.P.&L. steamer *Perth* and the tug *Princess Louise* passed, sounding their sirens in salute, and the Rev Andrew Forrest dedicated the lifeboat, 'To the service of humanity.' The Duchess of Montrose then christened her with the words, 'I name this boat *Mona,* and I pray God may bless and protect all who go out in her on her missions of mercy.'

Three weeks later, at 2.00 a.m. on 19 October, the *Mona* was launched when the sandboat *Oberon* was reported in difficulties in a full gale. The sandboat had run aground and it was almost 14 hours before the *Mona* could escort the *Oberon* into the Tidal Basin. The lifeboat was still in the harbour a short while later when the river steamer *Fair City* was reported in difficulties. The *Fair City* was very old and slow and quite unable to make any headway against the westerly gale. Jim Coull found her at anchor with her crew struggling to salvage their dinghy which had sunk alongside. After standing by the *Fair City* until it was clear that there was no immediate danger, the lifeboat returned to the harbour with a request from the *Fair City's* skipper, Alex Petrie, for a tug. *Fair City* eventually ran aground off the Stannergate and her crew walked ashore at low water.

The closing months of 1936 saw the beginning of the first regular television service. King Edward VIII abdicated, the press were reporting the romance between film star Katherine Hepburn and Howard Hughes, hunger marches were a common sight on Scottish streets and the International Brigade were about to play their part in that most bloody of conflicts, the Spanish Civil War. At 10.15 p.m. on Wednesday, 20 January 1937, Coxswain Coull had his wireless set tuned to the trawler waveband and heard a rather anxious voice say;

Abertay lightship calling. Hullo, hullo, anybody. Convey this message to Dundee Harbourmaster. Send lifeboat to stand by Abertay lightship.

An easterly storm had strewn fishing cobles and nets across Fisher Street and abnormally high spring tides meant that steamers in Camperdown Dock were riding so high that they appeared to be sitting on the quay. The strong winds and fierce tides had caused the lightship's mooring chains to become entangled with a submerged object and she was labouring heavily.

The *Mona* stood by the lightship for 16 hours until the weather moderated.

The lightship's mooring cable was still foul when another gale blew up ten days later. This time it parted and the lightship swung round until she was 700 feet off station. The *Mona* was launched into a blizzard at 12.25 p.m. and reached the lightship an hour later. Coxswain Coull was faced with the same problem that Coxswain Gall had encountered at the *Daydream* 18 years earlier; a small boat was hanging in davits over the leeward side of the wildly pitching lightship and would come crashing down onto the *Mona* as soon as she went alongside. Using the *Mona's* loudhailer, Coull told the lightship's crew to cut the boat away. A grappling hook was thrown and secured and, as Coull recalled later, 'Each succeeding wave carried the *Mona* up against the lightship, and each time we hit the ship, one of the lightshipmen jumped onto our foredeck.'* A cheering crowd greeted the lifeboat on her return to Broughty Ferry and Jim Coull was awarded a vellum presented by the Duke of Kent at the RNLI AGM in April 1937.

Coxswain Jim Coull brings the RNLB Mona *alongside at Broughty Ferry after the service to the Abertay lightship on the storm-lashed afternoon of Saturday, 30 January 1937. The five rescued lightshipmen can be seen lining the port side of the lifeboat. Standing next to the lifeboatman in white waders is the lightship's master, David Mearns. Almost 23 years later, on Tuesday, 8 December 1959, David Mearns, by then a senior coastguard based at Carnoustie, would be the first to go aboard the* Mona *after she capsized while answering a call to the North Carr lightship and was washed up on Buddon Sands.*

(DAVID ANGUS)

---

* The lightship's moorings had become entangled with the wreck of the steam tug *Protector*, sunk following a collision on 29 August 1889. She had been towing a brig upriver that evening but was unable to make any headway against a fast-running ebb tide. Captain Legg anchored at the side of the channel but, for some reason, did not show any lights. Another Dundee tug, the *Duncan,* had sailed that morning with a party of harbour trustees and their guests anxious to see that great wonder of the Victorian age, the new Forth Bridge. *Duncan* had dropped her passengers off at Burntisland, from where they returned home by rail, and was making her way back up the Tay channel at 10.20 p.m. when she ran straight into the unlit *Protector* and sank her.

The Dundee Fishing Company's steam trawler *Richmond Castle* developed a serious leak while fishing near the Bell Rock on Saturday, 29 January 1938. Skipper Alex Dorward set course for home but the pumps were unable to cope and she was beached near the mouth of Buddon Burn after the rising water reached her fires and she lost all power.

Two men went ashore by small boat to raise the alarm but the trawler's flares had already been seen by Buddon lightkeeper Charles Linness and the lifeboat was called out at 7.15 p.m. Signalman Syd Smith heard the maroons in church but was aboard the *Mona* as she got under way at 7.24 p.m. The trawler was lying on the sand with her decks awash and seven feet of water in her engine room. Rather optimistically, Skipper Dorward asked Jim Coull to radio Dundee Harbour for a tug but, as the tide rose, the trawler took on an alarming list to port and the eight men left aboard were taken off. The *Richmond* Castle was refloated the following month and taken to Granton for scrapping.

Coxswain Jim Coull, Motor Mechanic Johnny Grieve, Second Coxswain Jimmy Gall and the crew of the Mona *on Tuesday, 16 March 1937, wearing scarves knitted for them by a Mrs Manby of Codsall, Staffordshire. It had just been announced that Coull was to be awarded the Thanks of the RNLI inscribed on Vellum for the Abertay lightship service.*

Jim Coull was captured while serving in the Naval Brigade at Antwerp in 1914 and endured four years in a forced labour camp at Doebritz near Berlin. Along with three other POWs, he walked out of the camp in 1918, made his way to Hamburg and stowed away on a steamer. He returned to the sea as a fisherman and later on a coaster, before being appointed bowman of the Montrose lifeboat in 1930 and coxswain of the Broughty Ferry lifeboat in 1934.

The Mona's *exploits attracted considerable media attention and, on the evening of Friday, 28 May 1937, she was used to record the first outside broadcast from a lifeboat. The boat was launched trailing 180 feet of sound cable attached to a microphone strapped to BBC correspondent George Blake's chest. Great care had to be taken to ensure that the cable did not snap as the sound was being relayed direct to a recording studio in London. Entitled* Stormy Weather – The Launch of the Lifeboat, *the programme included interviews with Jim Coull and Johnny Grieve and was broadcast the following week.*
(DUNDEE COURIER AND EVENING TELEGRAPH)

The trawler Richmond Castle *developed a serious leak and was beached near the mouth of Buddon Burn on Saturday, 29 January 1938. Skipper Dorward and his crew were taken off by the Broughty Ferry lifeboat* Mona.
(DUNDEE COURIER AND EVENING TELEGRAPH)

On Saturday, 10 September 1938, Hitler was demanding territory from Czechoslovakia and air raid shelters were being dug in Scotland's parks. As Europe teetered on the brink of war, a crowd gathered that afternoon to watch the John and Sarah Hatfield *go down St Andrews harbour for the last time. David Fenton delivered the old lifeboat to her new owner, an Edinburgh yachtsman, the following day. A temporary reprieve from war was gained two weeks later at the Munich conference after which Prime Minister Neville Chamberlain boasted naively of 'Peace for our time'. As the yacht* Sarah John, *the* John and Sarah Hatfield *survived the coming war and was last seen still afloat in Cyprus in 1987.*
(ST ANDREWS UNIVERSITY PHOTOGRAPHIC COLLECTION)

Carnoustie coastguard station telephoned the Dundee Harbourmaster's office at 9.55 a.m. on Monday, 28 February 1938 with the news that a yawl was anchored in a dangerous position close to the Abertay lightship. Shortly afterwards, Charles Linness reported that he could see the yawl in difficulties in heavy seas. The *Mona* was launched at 11.00 a.m. and found the spratter *Sovereign* lying close to the banks. She had left Dundee the previous afternoon bound for Kincardine but her engine had broken down off Cellardyke so Jim Ross and new owner Allan McEwan decided to make sail and return to Dundee. A heavy sea was running as they crossed The Bar at dawn and a strong south-westerly gale prevented them reaching shelter on the Fife shore. They anchored off Buddon Ness but soon began to drag towards the Gaa Sands and were greatly relieved when the lifeboat hove into view. The *Mona* towed the *Sovereign* up river to the Tidal Basin.

Coxswain David Fenton of the St Andrews lifeboat was due to retire in September 1938. As at Broughty Ferry, there were few fishermen left in St Andrews and it was felt that nobody had the necessary experience to take over from him. With its tidal harbour and exposed beaches, St Andrews had never been an ideal launching site for a lifeboat. The modern motor lifeboats by then on station at Broughty Ferry, Anstruther and Arbroath had, in any case, rendered the 26 year-old old pulling and sailing lifeboat *John and Sarah Hatfield* obsolete. She had not been launched on service since standing by a disabled Aberdeen trawler, the *Ebor Abbey,* on 27 December 1932 and St Andrews Bay was no longer the trap it had been during the days of sail.

It was decided that St Andrews lifeboat station should close and, following a last exercise launch in August 1938, ropes and other gear belonging to the station were auctioned on Thursday, 1 September. David Fenton displayed the lots to a crowd that included both former crew members and souvenir hunters. It was a sad occasion, the end of an era, and the lots attracted little money. The oars failed to reach their reserve of 5/- (25p) and the carriage went to a local contractor for just £1.

In the 136 years since that cold January day in 1802 when Cathcart Dempster and Captain David Stewart first took the *Cork Lifeboat* out on exercise, lifeboats stationed at St Andrews and Boarhills had carried out well over 100 services and had saved more than 250 lives. One gold medal, eight silver medals and one bronze medal were awarded by the RNLI to St Andrews and Boarhills lifeboatmen.

Chapter Nine

THE MONA GOES TO WAR

The *Mona* carried out her last peacetime service on 19 December 1938 when the Finnish barque *Alastor,* running light from Plymouth for the Baltic with a crew of 15, was driven back across the North Sea from the Danish coast by easterly gales. Reaching the Scottish coast near Aberdeen, she made her way south in search of shelter only to find herself trapped at anchor close to the wreck of the *Uku* north of the Gaa Sands. Pilots aboard the cutter *John Plenderleith* reported her plunging and rolling in heavy seas and in imminent danger of going ashore. The *Mona* was launched at 9.02 a.m. and Coxswain Coull was asked to pick up Senior Pilot Captain Alex Cook from the *John Plenderleith* and put him aboard the *Alastor.* The barque was rolling heavily and Cook had to make a perilous leap from the lifeboat's deck to catch a rope ladder swinging from the barque's bows. The *Mona* passed a line from the tug *Harecraig* and the *Alastor* was towed up river to anchor in Stannergate Roads.

As described in Chapter One, the *Mona* went to war on 4 December 1939 when she searched for survivors of the torpedoed SS *Rudolf.* The service to the *Quixotic* and the search for the Icelandic trawler *Skallagrimur* took place on the 5th and 7th of December. On Tuesday, 12 December, Kapitanleutnant Heinz Scheringer brought the little *U13* in to the entrance to the Tay to sow a field of magnetic mines close to the fairway buoy.

Scheringer's mines claimed their first victim on the morning of Saturday, 6 January 1940 Captain Tom Knight, the master of the *John Plenderleith,* had just put Alex Cook aboard the inbound Ellerman jute liner *City of Marseilles* and was only 50 yards off her starboard side when a huge spout of water and mud erupted between the pilot cutter and the ship. The liner's engines stopped and she appeared at first to be settling. It was thought that the explosion could have been caused by a torpedo and, as a U boat might be lining up for another shot, Captain Olsen of the *City of Marseilles* gave the order to abandon ship. Two of the liner's lifeboats had been destroyed by the explosion and another capsized amid mounting chaos as her Lascar crew panicked and rushed the boats. Fourteen Lascars were pitched into the sea, one of whom died. Among the rescue craft that converged on the scene were the *Mona* and the RAF air-sea rescue launch from Tayport. As aircraft from Leuchars patrolled overhead, the *Mona* met the *John Plenderleith* coming up river towing the liner's lifeboats containing 163 survivors.

The survivors were landed at Broughty Ferry and taken to St James' Church Hall where they were fed and clothed by the village women who appeared every time the lifeboat went out. Many of the liner's crew had been dressing at the time of the explosion, some were almost naked and Rev Campbell went from door to door appealing for old clothing.

The *City of Marseilles* was still afloat at anchor south of the fairway buoy and, before the *Mona* was rehoused, Captain Olsen asked Jim Coull if he would take himself and some of his officers back out to her. When the lifeboat was used again the following day to put some of the liner's crew back aboard, many of them took one look at the *Mona* and refused point-blank to get aboard anything so small! The lifeboat passed a towing hawser and the tug *Harecraig* brought the *City of Marseilles* into Dundee for repair.

Enemy action of a different kind led to the next service for the *Mona* on Tuesday, 30 January 1940. Luftwaffe pilots showed remarkable tenacity in carrying out attacks against shipping off the east coast in all weathers. Heavy snow showers were falling over the Tay estuary that morning when the trawler *Lady Shirley* signalled that she was being attacked by a Heinkel bomber near the Bell Rock. The Ellerman liner *City of Bath* and the London steamer *Stancourt,* both waiting near the fairway buoy for the tide and a pilot, were next to be attacked. The City of Bath put up such a spirited anti-aircraft barrage that the bomber quickly shifted its attention to the *Stancourt.* The *Stancourt*'s crew were ordered below as the Heinkel dropped four bombs around her and strafed the decks with machine gun fire. One young lad from St Ives, on his first trip to sea, told a *Dundee Courier* reporter, 'When it power-dived over us and dropped a bomb, we just scrammed for cover.'

The master of the *Stancourt* attempted to run into the Tay for safety but, blinded by the snow, ran onto the northern edge Abertay Sands. The *Mona* was launched in reponse to her distress signals and, on their way down river, the lifeboatmen noticed that they were steaming through large quantities of wreckage. Coxswain Coull anchored the *Mona* to windward of the *Stancourt* and attempted to veer down onto the stranded steamer only for the lifeboat's anchor to drag. Eventually, the steamer shifted on the sands allowing the *Mona* just enough room to get alongside under her lee and take off her crew of 21. The first man to jump for the lifeboat missed his footing and had to be hauled, frozen, from the water. Again, on the way up river, the lifeboatmen saw a great deal of flotsam, among it wooden cases and barrels.

When the *Mona* returned to station, Coull found that the launchers had been unable to lay out the steadying ropes and anchors required in rehousing the boat. The lifeboat's own anchor was used instead and the crew returned to the boatshed at 1.00 a.m., when the tide had gone out, to recover it. On opening the large sliding doors they discovered a wooden case lying on the platform at the top of the slipway. It held six tins of ham, as Jim Coull recalled, 'Great brute tins, the shape o' a ham, you know, about ten pounds in every tin. Oh, this was a great capture, so we took that up into the shed.'

Looking along the moonlit beach, the lifeboatmen could see more flotsam lying on the tide line. By the old railway pier they came across a barrel marked 'Butter'. It was heavy and they were trying to work out how to get it back to the boatshed without rolling it, thus leaving a tell-tale trail in the snow, when a voice said, 'Hello, what's going on here?' The lifeboatmen looked up guiltily to see a policeman surveying the scene by the light of a shaded torch. As Jim Coull remembered, 'We a' kent him. We tell't him what it was and we tell't him our problem. He said, "See's a heave up wi' it," and we gave it a heave up onto his big broad shoulders and he carried it along to the boatshed. Ane o' our chaps went west instead o' east and he came back wi' a box full o' eggs.'

The crew of the steamer Stancourt *being landed at the Pilot Pier, Broughty Ferry, on the bitterly cold afternoon of Tuesday, 30 January 1940.* Stancourt *was one of three ships attacked that morning by enemy bombers while awaiting a pilot at the fairway buoy. Her master attempted to run the river on his own to seek safety but ran his ship onto the Abertay Bank in a blinding snowstorm. The* Mona *took off her crew and the* Stancourt *was refloated three weeks later.*
(DUNDEE COURIER AND EVENING TELEGRAPH)

By an uncanny coincidence, both bacon and butter had been placed on ration three weeks before, on 8 January. The next morning, when the lifeboatmen came down to the shed to divide the spoils, they found the beach crowded with locals intent on a share of the booty. Despite the bitter cold, women could be seen hoisting up their skirts and wading out into the water to grab cases of ham and children were taking away sledges, barrows, even prams loaded with barrels of butter. Not to be outdone, the lifeboatmen launched a small boat and salvaged what they could from the river. From Easthaven to the Craig Pier, the shoreline swarmed with people loading this latter-day manna from heaven into cars and onto horse-drawn carts.

It was not long before this attracted the attention of His Majesty's Receiver of Wrecks and the police were ordered to recover what they could, using the threat of prosecution if necessary. Lorries were sent round and some, but by no means all of the salvaged cargo was handed over. Motor Mechanic Johnny Grieve's daughter Vina remembers that she was heartily sick of the sight of ham before her family worked their way through their share. Over at Leuchars, the RAF hit upon a novel way of keeping officialdom away from cases of food that had washed up on the beach. They surrounded it with red flags and signs saying 'Danger - Mines'.* The *Stancourt* was refloated the following month and repaired in Dundee. Renamed the *Inaki*, she was lost off Cape Finisterre in 1942.

Kapitanleutnant Scheringer's mines claimed a second victim on 6 February 1940 when the little Estonian steamer *Anu* was blown apart while lying at anchor close to the fairway buoy. Six of her crew were killed and 13 survived a freezing night on rafts, finally drifting ashore at Carnoustie where they were found wandering about on the golf course by greenkeepers.

By the beginning of April 1941, Rommel's Afrika Korps was snapping at the heels of a British Army in headlong retreat towards Egypt. Britain's cities were reeling under the full fury of the blitz and much of Clydebank had just been reduced to smoking rubble in two massive raids which left 4,000 Clydesiders dead and injured. On the night of 3 April, six Heinkel III bombers of Kampfgeschwader 26 based in Norway attacked a convoy as it passed the Bell Rock. In the resulting confusion, the Belgian freighter *Emile Franqui* lost her course and struck the western edge of the Inchcape Reef. The *Mona* was launched to go to her aid and, after groping their way over The Bar at half speed in thick fog, the lifeboatmen made out the ghostly silhouette of a ship at anchor in the shallows south of the Abertay Sands.

Coxswain Coull anchored the *Mona* near the fairway buoy until daylight brought improved visibility. It transpired that the *Emile Franqui* had managed to free herself from the rocks only to come to anchor in an equally perilous position off the entrance to the river. Bumping heavily on the sandbanks, she had damaged her rudder and started to leak. Coull attempted to guide her out of the shallows only for the steamer to run aground again due to her damaged steering. The *Mona* landed eight passengers from the *Emile Franqui* at Broughty Ferry before returning to the steamer that evening in a nasty north-easterly wind to take off 37 of her crew. The officers elected to stay aboard until the steamer was towed away to the Forth for repair.

Broughty Ferry lifeboat station suffered its only war damage on Monday, 5 May 1941. The *Mona* was about to leave that morning for Grangemouth, the Forth and Clyde Canal, and a refit at Robertson's boatyard at Sandbank in the Holy Loch. Police Constable Robert Stirrat had been ordered to stand guard over a mine which had been washed up on the beach opposite the bottom of Dundas Street, just west of the boatshed. For some reason, just after 6.00 a.m., Stirrat tied a rope to the mine and started to drag it up the beach. More than 50 years later, one Fisher Street resident could still recall hearing a clanking sound followed by an explosion which blew in all her windows. Dozens of windows were shattered, including those in the boatshed. Flying pebbles drilled neat holes in fishing boats, slates were stripped from roofs and splinters were found embedded in the interior walls of cottages. Robert Stirrat died that afternoon in Dundee Royal Infirmary.

---

* Exactly which wreck was the source of the food is not known, though one possible candidate is the Norwegian steamer *Pluto* which was torpedoed off the east coast by the *U19* on 23 January 1940. among the debris washed up on Carnoustie beach was a liferaft bearing her name.

Effective lifeboat services recorded on the station service boards are only those where lives are saved or assistance is given. Numerous launches turn out to be either false alarms, hoaxes or occasions when the lifeboat is not required and are not recorded on the service boards. One such case was recalled by Coxswain Jim Coull as one of his worst experiences at sea.

It began on the evening of Sunday, 9 November 1941, when the Admiralty tug *Buccaneer* was riding out a near gale off the entrance to Montrose. She had an unwieldy battle-practice target* in tow but could not enter harbour as huge seas were breaking over the narrow channel between Scurdie Ness and the Annat Bank. Scurdie Ness lighthouse was often used as a landfall by enemy bombers and, at 6.15 pm, a single Heinkel 111 bombed and strafed the *Buccaneer.* One bomb passed through the tug's deck and out through her side without exploding, near misses disabled her engine and a small fire was started by tracer bullets.

As the battered tug drifted ashore at the mouth of the North Esk, the Montrose lifeboat *The Good Hope* was launched to her aid. Due to the black-out, it was completely dark and, after a hair-raising trip across the bar at the harbour entrance, the Montrose lifeboatmen could see nothing. The *Buccaneer*'s crew were taken safely ashore by breeches buoy and, as the weather had worsened, there was no possibility of the lifeboat getting back into Montrose so *The Good Hope's* crew made for the open sea to await daylight. Their wireless had broken down, a common fault with the early sets fitted to lifeboats.

Coastguards, unable to contact *The Good Hope,* became increasingly concerned for her safety and telephoned Jim Coull in Broughty Ferry at regular intervals during the night. As a former Montrose lifeboatman, Coull knew that *The Good Hope* would have made for the open sea rather than dodge about close inshore. In those pre-radar days, there was little the Broughty Ferry lifeboat could do on a dark, gale-lashed winter's night. Shortly before dawn, however, the *Mona* put to sea and, on reaching Montrose Bay, Coxswain Coull and his crew could see the tug and target lying in the breakers, too far inshore for the lifeboat to get close. As with *The Good Hope,* the *Mona*'s wireless had broken down; they could hear Dundee Harbour and the coastguard station at Fife Ness, but could speak to nobody.

The censor has obliterated the Mona's *name in this undated wartime photograph. The lifeboat's wartime equipment muster included a rifle though Coxswain Jim Coull was never entirely sure why it was there.*
(DUNDEE COURIER AND EVENING TELEGRAPH)

---

* Battle practice targets were pontoons fitted with large lattice-work targets and moored in Lunan Bay. They were used for gunnery practice by trainee fighter pilots but marksmanship was notoriously bad and the target often escaped entirely unscathed while other aircraft, even ground staff, occasionally suffered damage.

In the early afternoon, as the Broughty Ferry lifeboatmen searched northwards towards Johnshaven for their missing colleagues, *The Good Hope* was swamped while making a desperate attempt to get through the mountainous breakers at the entrance to Montrose. Her coxswain and two of her crew were washed overboard but were fortunately still alive when found on the sands.

The weather worsened steadily as the afternoon wore on, and visiblity deteriorated as it grew darker. Still unaware of the fate of the Montrose lifeboat, the Broughty Ferry men realised that they would have to look to their own safety and set out for home. The only sight of land they got on the way south from Montrose was a brief glimpse of Red Head at the south end of Lunan Bay. The seas became even wilder as they closed the Tay Bar and Jim Coull recalled thinking, 'If we see the fairway buoy, we'll run The Bar. If we dinna, we'll nae begin tae look for it.' He knew that, once committed to the river, there would be no turning back.

A sounding was taken by lead line and it was found that, despite being in 12 fathoms (22 metres) of water, and well out from The Bar, the sea was still breaking very heavily. All thoughts of getting back into the Tay were abandoned and Coull set a course for the south and shelter under the lee of the Isle of May in the Forth. The lights on the Bell Rock and the Isle of May were blacked out and the North Carr lightship had been removed. The only beacon left to guide the *Mona* into the Forth was a dimmed red light on a small buoy put in place of the North Carr. The faint glow from this light was seen and Coull brought the *Mona* safely into shelter west of the Isle of May.

By now the *Mona* had been at sea for almost 18 hours and, to the considerable anxiety of the crew's families, unable to communicate with anyone. The lifeboatmen tried repeatedly, but unsuccessfully, to attract the attention of the small military garrison on the Isle of May. Coull knew that anchoring in that position would be most unwise as there were usually loose mines floating about in bad weather. Entering a harbour at night in wartime was strictly forbidden but the *Mona's* fuel situation was becoming critical and he decided that they must run up the Forth for Granton. After crossing to the south shore of the river in search of sheltered water, and with all their navigation lights switched on, they shaped a course for the anti-submarine boom that stretched across the river at Inchkeith.

The winch wire takes the strain as the Mona *is rehoused after an exercise in May 1953. The bottom of the slipway was forever being blocked by shingle and groynes were constructed west of the boatshed in 1926 in an effort to deal with the problem. These were removed in 1958 as they did little to reduce the build up of shingle and the exposed posts presented a considerable hazard to the lifeboat during rehousing. On one occasion, a bulldozer hired to push the shingle out into the river at low tide suffered brake failure and launched itself into the river, much to the astonishment of its driver.*

(DUNDEE COURIER AND EVENING TELEGRAPH)

Suddenly, a signal lamp flashed out, 'What Ship?' The *Mona*'s crew replied that they were the Broughty Ferry lifeboat and that they desperately needed to get through the gate in the boom and up to Granton as their fuel was almost exhausted. The boom patrol vessel replied that the boom was closed and that the lifeboat must steer north-west for Methil. Groping forward through the darkness, Coull recalled that, 'The first thing we saw was a whitening, nae a light but something a bitty lighter than the darkness, and I thought,'We're right on Methil here because that'll be them working the little engines that they have on Methil pier for the coal.'It looked like the glare from the opening o' a fire and we eased the boat down, dead slow, until we made out what it was.'

It became abruptly clear that the 'whitening' was caused by spray from waves crashing against Methil breakwater. The engines were put hard astern and only the vigilance of her crew saved the *Mona* from being smashed to pieces. Jim Coull, who had been at the wheel for more than 14 hours, reversed course a short way and anchored until daybreak. Only then did the lifeboatmen discover that, as they approached Methil in the darkness, they had steamed right through a densely packed convoy of blacked-out ships lying at anchor. The *Mona* was refuelled in Methil that morning and returned to Broughty Ferry after a service lasting nearly 36 hours.

On another occasion during the war, the *Mona* was launched to a Soviet steamer reported in distress off the Bell Rock. Arbroath and Montrose lifeboats could not be launched due to severe weather conditions. The *Mona* reached the last reported position of the Soviet steamer but found nothing and set course for home. As she followed a submarine bound for HMS *Ambrose,* the Dundee naval base, over The Bar, her searchlight was torn from its mounting and washed up on the beach at Carnoustie. The Soviet ship had been nowhere near the Bell Rock. The *Mona's* last wartime service took place on 28 April 1945 when she rescued two men from the fishing boat *Annie* in difficulties off Westhaven.

Dundee in 1948 was still a grim-faced industrial city with thousands of industrial and domestic chimneys pouring smoke into an already heavily polluted atmosphere. Mixed with warm, damp air over a cold sea, this formed the sort of impenetrable smog that is now only a distant, unpleasant memory. Just such a 'pea-souper' had settled over the Tay on the evening of Wednesday, 1 December, as the ferry *Sir William High* groped her way across from Newport into the Craig Harbour with a full load of cars and passengers. The only 'Fifie' not equipped with radar, she missed the harbour entrance and lurched onto the Fowler Rock at 7.06 p.m. SOS signals were sounded on her siren and oddly disembodied voices shouted across to her from the harbour wall just 80 yards away.

The ferry passengers thought the whole thing a huge joke and, as crewmen lowered a lead line over the side to check the depth of water, one shouted, 'Look, they're catching fish for our breakfast.' Harbour officials, however, failed to see the funny side; the tide was ebbing and they were concerned at what might happen should the ferry's cargo shift. The *Mona* was launched at 7.15 p.m. but took 40 minutes to find the stranded ferry as visibility had closed in to only about 50 feet. The lifeboat took off 40 passengers on the first run, landing them at the Camperdown Lockway at 8.30 p.m. Another 30 passengers were landed on the second run and the lifeboat then put harbour officials aboard the ferry before returning to station. The ferry floated off on the tide shortly after midnight.

In January 1952 the *Mona* took Skipper Fred Potter and his crew of three off the sand boat *David P* which was listing in a strong gale close to the entrance to Camperdown Dock. That March she undertook a seven hour search for the crew of the Swedish steamer *Rosso* which had foundered in a gale east of Fife Ness. Nothing was found.

At 9.15 p.m. on 26 October 1953 the *Islandmagee* of the Tay Sand Co. was seen in difficulties as she passed the North Carr lightship in a violent south-easterly gale bound for Leith. Flares were seen shortly afterwards and, with great difficulty, Anstruther and Arbroath lifeboats were launched to her aid. The *Islandmagee* was lost with her crew of six and the Arbroath lifeboat *Robert Lindsay* capsized while returning to harbour early the following morning. Six of her crew died and the sole survivor, Archie Smith, was rescued when a rocket

Coxswain Jim Coull, Motor Mechanic Johnny Grieve and the Mona's *crew in 1953. Bowman George Watson is wearing the white waders and, at his left shoulder, is Second Coxswain George Smith. Johnny Grieve, George Smith and George Watson lost their lives in the* Mona *disaster in 1959.*
(DUNDEE COURIER AND EVENING TELEGRAPH)

line, fired desperately into the darkness, landed across him.

Jim Coull retired in June 1956. One of his last launches as coxswain had taken place at the beginning of December 1955 when, for the first time, the *Mona* exercised with one of the new air-sea rescue helicopters based at RAF Leuchars. The early helicopters were primitive but they soon became an indispensable part of the rescue services and remain so today.

Chapter Ten

TELL DAVE THE BOAT'S GOING OUT

North Carr Light Vessel broken adrift and drifting in a north-westerly direction.
Advise launch.
(TELEPHONE MESSAGE FROM CARNOUSTIE COASTGUARDS AT 2.42 A.M., TUESDAY, 8 DECEMBER 1959)

It was cold, bitterly cold. Weak, leaden daylight struggled through a blanket of grey-black cloud and breakers thundered in from the North Sea to pound themselves into boiling foam on the beach. An easterly gale drove rain and sleet before it in squalls that stung the eyes and blurred the horizon. Bill Philip surveyed the lonely, windswept desolation of Buddon Ness, shrugged his shoulders deeper into his coat, called his dog to heel and walked on.

At first, from Barry Burn, the boat surging backwards and forwards in the surf looked just like a ship's boat cast ashore by the storm. As he got closer, however, he could make out the gold lettering on her blue hull; RNLB MONA - BROUGHTY FERRY LIFEBOAT. A single red navigation light glared eerily from her bow and a sodden seaman's jersey hung from her rail.

Twice he called out, but the only reply came from the seagulls that screamed mournfully as they wheeled and dived overhead. A few yards away, at the water's edge, waves were breaking over the oilskin-clad body of a young man. On that miserable Tuesday morning, the 8th of December 1959, Bill Philip was the first witness to one of the worst lifeboat disasters to strike the Scottish coast.

December 1959 was more than just the last month of the decade. The Mini had been launched that summer and Britain's first motorway, the M1, had just opened. The economy was booming, unemployment was almost non-existent and, claiming that the country had never had it so good, Prime Minister Harold Macmillan's Conservative government had been returned to power with an increased majority in the October general election. The nation was becoming addicted to ever more numerous television sets and popular programmes of the day included *Emergency Ward 10, No Hiding Place* and *Crackerjack*. The film comedy *Genevieve* was packing them in at the Dundee Odeon, though the cinema hit of the year had been *Ben Hur.* Radio favourites included *The Navy Lark, Mrs Dale's Diary,* and *Hancock's Half Hour.* Perry Como, Ruby Murray and Russ Conway all had Christmas records in the hit parade and, on Wednesday, 2 December, screaming girls tried to stop Cliff Richard leaving a concert at Dundee's Gaumont Theatre by throwing themselves under the wheels of his car.

Dundee Branch of the RNLI held its annual general meeting two days later on Friday, 4 December, and welcomed a new coxswain for the *Mona* in 29 year-old Ronnie Grant. Under the watchful eye of RNLI District Engineer Alex Cursiter, Grant took the *Mona* out on exercise the following afternoon. Originally from Tayport, he had gone to sea as a boy seaman with the Ben Line and subsequently had a spell as a boatswain with the Dundee, Perth and London line. He left the sea in 1957 and took a job in the Caledon Shipyard.

The *Dundee Courier* for Monday, 7 December, carried an item on the test borings that were about to begin along the line of the proposed Tay Road Bridge. The lead story, however, was an account of the furious storm that had swept in from the North Atlantic over the weekend. Under the headline 'Sea Tragedy' there was a report on the loss, with all hands, of the Aberdeen trawler *George Robb* near Duncansby Head. Two ships were reported sinking off the Norwegian coast, a Finnish steamer was ashore near Fraserburgh and the Cunard liner *Queen Elizabeth* was steaming towards Cherbourg with shattered portholes, flooded cabins and several injured passengers.

Closer to home, a trail of devastation had been wrought along the Angus coastline. Hundreds of power and telephone cables had been brought down, rivers had burst their banks, fallen trees had blocked roads and sand-drifts four feet high had formed on Broughty Ferry Esplanade and the railway embankment at Carnoustie. Several ships were storm-bound in Dundee and, as waves were breaking right inside the Craig Harbour, the Tay Ferries were moored overnight at Newport Pier.

Off Fife Ness, the 500,000 candlepower light of the North Carr lightship flashed out twice every 30 seconds across an angry, empty sea. Captain George Rosie and his six crewmen had settled down for another uncomfortable night, pitching and rolling in the exceptionally heavy seas when, at 2.02 a.m., the lightship's main anchor chain parted, setting her adrift and helpless before the storm.

Ronnie Grant (above) was appointed the Mona's coxswain in November 1959. His predecessor, ex-Coxswain Alex Gall, offered to accompany Coxswain Grant on his first few services to give him the benefit of his many years of lifeboat experience.
(DUNDEE COURER AND EVENING TELEGRAPH)

Gusts of over 50 mph were buffeting the coastguard lookout at Fife Ness where Charlie Jones had just climbed up to relieve Bruce Burgess on watch. The two men were having a cup of tea a few minutes later when Burgess spotted the lightship moving off station. Coastguard District Officer Joe Levitt was informed by telephone and he immediately asked for the Arbroath and Anstruther lifeboats. Neither was able to launch as it was almost dead low water and that combined with the severe south-easterly gale had rendered both harbour entrances impassable. Levitt then contacted Carnoustie coastguard station to ask for the only available lifeboat, the *Mona*. The message was passed to Dundee Harbourmaster Norman Moug at 2.42 a.m. and he in turn telephoned Ronnie Grant and Motor Mechanic Johnny Grieve.

In the lifeboat mechanic's house at 135 Fisher Street, Johnny Grieve roused his 22 year-old son John, a regular member of the *Mona*'s crew since 1956, and the two men dressed hurriedly. While his father crossed to the boatshed to fire the maroons, John ran round to crewman David Anderson's house in King Street, knocked on the window and shouted 'Tell Dave the boat's going out.' Norman Moug saw the maroons exploding as he drove to the boatshed. He arrived at 3.10 a.m. to find that Ronnie Grant and his crew had assembled and Head Launcher Charlie Knight was preparing the *Mona* for launching. Moug recalled that things went very smoothly and quietly as the crew made ready and the lifeboat roared down the slipway for the last time three minutes later.

The *Mona*'s crew rigged their signal mast and passed their first message to Fife Ness coastguard station at 3.20 a.m. At 3.36 a.m., Charlie Jones called the lifeboat with the message, 'North Carr is on the air now, you can get them if you give them a call.' The *Mona* was unable to raise the lightship and, at 3.53 a.m., Jones called the lifeboat again to say, 'North Carr has just fired a rocket. Did you see it?' The lifeboat replied that they had not, and asked for the position of the lightship. They were told that the North Carr was riding to her spare bower anchor two miles north by west of Fife Ness and was firing rockets at regular intervals. Jones also told the lifeboat that a searchlight was being set up on Fife Ness to give them a bearing.

Despite the appalling weather, the *Mona* made her way down river at six knots and, at about 4.00 a.m., Senior Coastguard David Mearns got his first sight of her as she cleared Buddon Ness. Mearns said later that she appeared to have reduced speed and was constantly disappearing from view behind mountainous seas. At 4.06 a.m., Charlie Jones asked the lifeboat, 'What is your position now please?' The *Mona* replied, 'Our position now is just abeam of the Abertay lightship.'

Watched by David Mearns, the lifeboat plunged on through the huge waves crashing over The Bar. The North Carr fired another distress rocket at 4.25 a.m. and, from Fife Ness, Jones signalled the *Mona* to ask if they had seen it. In the violently lurching lifeboat, the radio operator was only able to gasp out in reply, 'No...our position...we have just passed the middle buoys on The Bar and we are just hanging on.'

Mearns saw the lifeboat turn south into St Andrews Bay at about 4.45 a.m. At 4.48 a.m., Charles Jones signalled to the *Mona*, 'North Carr has just fired a red rocket. Did you see it?' The *Mona*'s last message was, 'Yes, we saw that one. We have just cleared The Bar.' Norman Moug telephoned Fife Ness at 5.08 a.m. to find that contact with the lifeboat had been lost. The Northern Lighthouse tender *Pharos* lying in Granton tried to raise the lifeboat at 5.10 a.m. but their signal also went unanswered.

The *Mona*'s wireless set had clearly failed but Fife Ness coastguards saw her masthead light in St Andrews Bay at 5.39 a.m.* They were unable to estimate how far away she was but Jones immediately signalled the lightship, 'Do you see the ship's lights approaching you now bearing 332 degrees Fife Ness?' They replied, 'Yes, I think it is the lifeboat. Will burn another flare.' Jones then signalled the lifeboat on 2182 kcs, the distress frequency, 'Your transmitter seems to have broken down. If your receiver is working, fire rockets and flash your searchlight up in the sky.' He got no response and the lights disappeared a few minutes later.

Concern for the lifeboat mounted as the night wore on and, just after 8.00 a.m., a Bristol Sycamore helicopter of 228 Squadron took off from Leuchars to search for her. Flight Sergeant Clarke saw the lightship at anchor in heavy seas off the Fife coast. The spare anchor cable on which she had been lying parted at 6.30 a.m., setting her adrift again. Captain Rosie's men then dropped their last spare anchor, slowly paying out 140 fathoms of cable until she was lying just over a mile off Boarhills.

Clarke said later, 'We had a look at the Tay estuary and then went over as far as the lifeboat station at Broughty Ferry. We tried to make contact with the lifeboat, but failed. We went across to Fife Ness and found the North Carr in her new position.' The helicopter then returned to Leuchars, refuelled and took off again with orders to search the coast at Buddo Ness between St Andrews and Boarhills. As Clarke recalled, 'This was not a mistake for Buddon Ness, but it was the new position of the lightship, and it must have been that someone had mistaken the lightship for the lifeboat.'

Bill Philip had already reached the *Mona* when, in the half light at about 8.45 a.m., David Mearns saw her rocking in the surf and the maroons were fired to call out the rocket brigade. John Hamilton had just arrived at work after being on auxiliary coastguard duty for most of the night. Hearing the maroons, he cycled back to the coastguard station but found it deserted. A scribbled note stating that the *Mona* was ashore on Buddon Sands was lying on a desk.

---

* The navigation lights could only have been those of the *Mona* as she and the lightship were the only vessels in St Andrews Bay that night.

Mearns made his way round by car, calling at Carnoustie police station on the way. Hamilton went along the beach and arrived first, just in time to help Bill Philip pull the young man's body out of the surf.

The North Carr lightship came to her last spare anchor off Kingsbarns at 6.45 a.m. on Tuesday, 8 December, two hours before the Mona *was discovered on Buddon Sands. The Northern Lighthouse tender MV* Pharos *and the Admiralty salvage tug* Earner *tried to get a line aboard the lightship that afternoon but were beaten by the weather. Further attempts to secure a tow failed and two air-sea rescue helicopters from RAF Leuchars had to fly within five feet of the wildly swaying lantern to take off her crew at lunchtime on 9 December.*
A tow was finally secured at 11.30a.m. on Friday, 11 December, just as the memorial service for the crew of the Mona *was ending in Broughty Ferry. The lightship was towed to Leith for repair and was put back on station on 16 March 1960. Withdrawn in the mid 1970s, she spent almost 20 years as a museum ship in Anstruther Harbour before moving to Dundee's Victoria Dock in 1995.*
(DUNDEE COURIER AND EVENING TELEGRAPH)

News of the sighting was flashed to the helicopter and, at about 9.10 a.m., Flight Sergeant Clarke found the *Mona* sitting upright in the surf with waves breaking over her. A small knot of people was gathering on the sand. Master Signaller Jacobs was winched down on a wildly swinging wire until he was hanging just over the lifeboat. He said later, 'I did not go into the boat, but I could see five bodies in it. A sixth body had been washed up on the beach.'

The *Mona* settled into the sand as the tide began to recede and, at 9.20 a.m., Mearns ran out behind a retreating wave and hauled himself aboard. Opening the cabin hatch, he shouted down, 'Is anybody there?' He got no reply but noticed that the cabin was in a state of some confusion and that around a foot of water covered the floor.

Making his way aft, he found the five bodies in the cockpit. David Anderson was at the after end, under the steering shaft. Ronnie Grant lay just in front of the wheel which, seemingly directed by his dead hands, was being spun to and fro by the waves hitting the rudder. Jim Ferrier and George Smith were slumped against the engine room bulkhead and, as though in a last, despairing attempt at escape, Johnny Grieve had his head and shoulders through the open engine room hatch. The young man's body on the beach was that of his son, John.

This was a particularly poignant moment for David Mearns. Not only did he know all of the dead men, he had also been in command of the Abertay lightship in January 1937 when one of her mooring chains had parted and Jim Coull brought the *Mona* alongside to rescue her crew. Mearns was struck by how little damaged the lifeboat appeared. About ten feet of the starboard railing and footwhale had been bent inwards and the centre section of the windscreen was missing along with four ventilator cowls. The signal mast had broken off just above the tabernacle. Police Inspector James Middleton arrived soon afterwards with the news that the mast had been found on the beach about half a mile south towards Buddon Ness. Lying next to it was the body of ex-Coxswain Alex Gall. Of Bowman George Watson there was no sign, though his lifejacket was later washed up on the beach.

For the wives left behind at Broughty Ferry, the night had been one long, anxious wait for news. Mary Grieve sat up listening to the exchange of wireless messages and became alarmed when the coastguards lost contact with the *Mona*. She telephoned the Harbour Chambers shortly after 9.30 a.m. only to be given the shocking news that both her husband and her son were dead. Charlotte Ferrier felt uneasy when she opened the blinds and saw ex-Coxswain Jim Coull talking to a policeman in Fisher Street. She went to the boatshed but was told that the *Mona* was safe and sheltering in St Andrews Bay for the night. Shortly afterwards, in Ambrose Street, she met George Smith's sister who told her that the lifeboat was lost. Both women went to see Mary Grieve and were handed a glass of brandy before being told the full extent of the tragedy.

Lexie Anderson had gone back to bed only to waken at 6.00 a.m. with the feeling that something terrible had happened. She got up and walked down Fort Street to the boatshed but was told that all was well. She did not learn the truth until almost 11.00 a.m. when she overheard people in the street talking about the *Mona* and ran back to the boatshed. Winnie

The Mona *settling into the sand at Buddon on the evening after the disaster. The damage to the starboard rail caused when she rolled upright in the breakers is clearly visible.*

Alick Mackay, then motor mechanic of the Arbroath lifeboat and later coxswain at Broughty Ferry, was one of the first to go aboard the Mona *on Buddon Sands. The bodies of the dead crewmen had just been removed and, as he examined the lifeboat's machinery, he found poignant vestigates of humanity scattered about the after cockpit; some odd socks, a pair of carpet slippers, a red lifeboat scarf, a coat, a jacket and a sou'wester.*

The coat, jacket and sou'wester he tied down over the holes left by the missing ventilator cowls and he lashed the wheel to stop the rudder thrashing backwards and forwards. The boat's anchor and drogue were then laid out to stop any further movement.

(DUNDEE COURIER AND EVENING TELEGRAPH)

Watson was at work as a nurse at the Armitstead Home when the news was broken to her. Josephine Grant heard the news on the radio before anyone reached her home in Cotton Road, Dundee.

The *Evening Telegraph's* Pat Shearer was one of a number of reporters sent out to likely points when the *Mona* was first reported missing. He was already at the Pilot Pier in Broughty Ferry when, shortly before 10.00 a.m., he heard that the lifeboat had been found. Driving out to Buddon, he ignored the red flag flying on the gunnery range and got to the beach just as the last body was being brought ashore.

News of the disaster simply stunned Broughty Ferry. Ashen-faced men and women gathered around the empty lifeboat shed, shivering in the cold and rain as they waited for news. Visitors to the homes of the dead crewmen included Rev Malcolm Ritchie, the minister of St James' Church, Norman Moug and Captain William Keay, President of the Dundee Branch of the RNLI. Conversation in the Gray Street cafes was muted and shop windows gaily decorated for Christmas suddenly seemed wholly inappropriate.

Lord Provost Hughes announced the opening of a Disaster Fund with a donation from Dundee Corporation of £2,000. Ronnie Grant, Jim Ferrier, Alex Gall and John Grieve had all worked at the Caledon Shipyard and a sizeable early contribution from them helped the fund reach over £14,000 within 48 hours. Staff at the City Chambers worked far into the night to cope with the flood of donations which ranged from 2/- (10p) to £500. One envelope was found to contain 100 sixpences and a note in a child's handwriting that said simply, 'Susan's six-month saving of sixpences.' Another donation came anonymously from Rome.

More than £270 was collected at performances of Gilbert and Sullivan's *Princess Ida* which was being presented that week in Dundee's Palace Theatre by Broughty Operatic Society. One of the principals was George Smith's 22 year-old son Sydney who carried on in the role despite his father's death. Tickets for a fund-raising concert in Green's Playhouse sold out in less than two hours. Among the many Scottish entertainers who gave their services were tenor Canon Sydney MacEwan, Jimmy Shand, Dennis Clancy, Robert Wilson and a young Sydney Devine. The *Mona* disaster touched the nation's conscience and, by the time the fund finally closed in 1960, it had reached over £90,000.

Mourners gathering outside St James' Kirk for the memorial service for the crew of the Mona *on the morning of Friday, 11 December 1959.*
(DUNDEE COURIER AND EVENING TELEGRAPH)

Crowds began to gather outside St James' Church at 9.30 a.m. on Friday, 11 December, an hour before the memorial service was due to begin. The fishermen's kirk held only around 400 so the service was relayed to another 300 seated in St James' Hall and hundreds more lining the street outside. Among those standing in the wind and rain were lifeboatmen from Anstruther, Montrose and Arbroath, RAF personnel from Leuchars and a party of coastguards led by David Mearns. Shops and offices closed, blinds were drawn, the streets emptied of traffic and a hush fell over the village as the dead men's families arrived in small groups at the church. Hymn 556, *Be still my soul,* was sung to Sibelius' hauntingly evocative *Finlandia* as two RAF jet fighters, only fleetingly visible through the murk, thundered overhead in salute.

The first funeral left Alex Gall's home in David Street shortly after the end of the memorial service. The coffin, covered with an RNLI flag, was almost hidden under a mountain of wreaths. A group of men joined the cortege as it passed the lifeboat houses at the corner of David Street and Fisher Street. They followed as the hearse wound its way slowly through the rainswept streets to Barnhill Cemetery where more than 200 mourners gathered to pay their last respects. The saddest event of that melancholy day, the double funeral for Johnny Grieve and his son held in a packed Dundee Crematorium, was followed by the cremation of George Smith. Ronnie Grant was interred at the Eastern Cemetery, then many of the mourners returned to Barnhill Cemetery for the funerals of Jim Ferrier and David Anderson.

It was an emotionally drained Branch Committee that gathered in the Harbour Chambers that evening to discuss the tragedy and its consequences for the station. Broughty Ferry's importance as an all-weather lifeboat station capable of operating at all states of the tide was underlined by RNLI representatives who stated that they would send a relief lifeboat as soon as a crew could be found to man her. Honorary Secretary Andrew Young was able to report that he had already received 13 written applications and a number of verbal requests to join a new crew.

The *Mona,* meanwhile, was still lying on the sand at Buddon. Firemen had manhandled a portable pump 300 yards across the beach to remove almost 10 tons of water from her flooded compartments. The Arbroath lifeboat *Duke of Montrose* attempted to tow her off on Sunday, 13 December, but the *Mona* was deeply embedded in the sand and only moved around 50 yards before she again stuck fast. Coxswain Henry Smith brought the *Duke of Montrose* right into the breakers the following afternoon, pulled the *Mona* free of the sands and secured her in Arbroath Harbour for the night. Once again towed by the *Duke of Montrose,* she slipped out of Arbroath early the following morning bound for Weatherhead's Shipyard at Cockenzie.

Once at Weatherhead's, the *Mona* was fully surveyed. It was clear that she had capsized but the investigators were trying to identify when, where and why this had happened. She had used 15 gallons of petrol which gave a running time of between two hours at full speed and three and a half hours at half speed. This implied that she must have capsized between 5.15 a.m. and 6.45 a.m. The last message had been received from her at 4.48 a.m., but she had been sighted from Fife Ness at 5.39 a.m. A watch found in Alex Gall's pocket had stopped just after 6.19 a.m., though it was felt that water would have taken some minutes to penetrate his clothing and the watch case. Neither of the boat's clocks were of any help; one was still running and the other had stopped prior to launching. Taking all this into consideration, it would appear that the disaster occurred sometime between 5.39 a.m. and 6.00 a.m.

The lifeboat had signalled that she was clear of The Bar at 4.48 a.m. and, when she was sighted from Fife Ness some 50 minutes later, visibility was recorded as being approximately four miles, reducing to two miles in rain showers. All the indications are that she was running at half ahead and, assuming a broadly similar pattern of drift to that of the fairway buoy which broke loose at about the same time, this suggests that the capsize took place around two miles south of The Bar.

That the appalling weather conditions had been the root cause of the disaster was beyond doubt. There remained the question of whether a failure of any of the *Mona's* equipment had been a contributory cause and a number of thorny problems presented themselves to the Fatal Accident Enquiry held in Dundee on Wednesday, 24 February 1960. Why was there so much water in the cabin? Why had George Watson taken off his lifejacket? Why was Johnny Grieve in the engine room with the hatch open?

Jim Coull had been the *Mona*'s coxswain for 21 years and his evidence must be treated with respect. Both cabin ventilator cowls were missing as were two of the three ventilator cowls from the engine room casing. Coull believed that the missing cowls pointed to the true cause of the disaster and that they had been swept off as the *Mona* fought her way over The Bar, thus allowing water into the boat.

There is some circumstantial evidence to support the theory that water had been getting into the *Mona* before she capsized. It is certainly possible that water had caused the radio to fail perhaps as much as an hour earlier. In addition, while George Watson's body was never found, his lifejacket was washed up on the beach, his jacket and sou-wester were in the cockpit and his pullover was hanging from the port railing. He would have had to remove his lifejacket before taking off his jacket and pullover which he may have been about to use in an attempt to block missing ventilators, possibly those on the engine room. Jim Coull was adamant that something must have been very wrong for Johnny Grieve to open up the engine room in such a violent storm.

Whatever happened, the *Mona* did capsize and, as the engine room hatch was open, air from that compartment vented through the cockpit drains allowing the upturned boat to settle low in the water. George Watson was probably thrown clear while the rest of the crew were trapped. Still inverted, she was carried north-west past the end of the Abertay Sands and across the shallows north of the Gaa Sands where the masthead touched bottom and the mast broke off at the tabernacle. Along with Alex Gall's body, it was carried ashore half a mile south of the lifeboat. The *Mona* was rolled upright in the breakers, crushing her windscreen and bending her starboard rail in the process. John Grieve's body was swept out and washed up onto the beach nearby.

Sheriff Christie spoke for many when he said at the end of the Fatal Accident Enquiry;

We have it on the authority of St John the Evangelist that greater love hath no man than this, than that a man lay down his life for his friends. That is the highest standard and that is the standard that those men reached. It seems to me that when men do reach that standard, not only in their thoughts, but in their deeds and actions, they are beyond the realm of comment from lesser men like us.

The jury returned a formal verdict.

The *Mona* lay stripped and forgotten in Cockenzie. Her last voyage began when she was pulled across the harbour on the night of Thursday, 17 March 1960. In the early hours of the following morning, she was moved round the breakwater, secured with two chains and allowed to dry out on the rocky foreshore. It was still dark at 4.30 a.m. when petrol was poured into her, a lighted brand was thrown and she exploded into flame. The *Mona* died in secret and, by daybreak, all that was left of her was a charred stern post and twisted metal bulkheads.

The decision to burn the *Mona* attracted much hostility and sadness, not just among lifeboatmen. Jim Coull said later, 'What a horrible end for a boat that did her duty. She did not deserve that.' Others felt that burning her was a waste of a perfectly seaworthy boat, though this was usually based on inflated estimates of her value. The funeral pyre of the *Mona* was blamed for a £40,000 drop in legacies to the RNLI in 1960 alone.

Chapter Eleven

SPIRIT OF TAYSIDE

The relief lifeboat *City of Bradford II* arrived at Broughty Ferry on Tuesday, 22 December 1959. Denis Wicksteed, the RNLI District Inspector, exercised the boat with her new crew the following afternoon, then telephoned headquarters in London to tell them that, just two weeks after the *Mona* disaster, Broughty Ferry lifeboat station was once again fully operational.

The relief lifeboat City of Bradford II *arrived at Broughty Ferry on the afternoon of Tuesday, 22 December 1959, just two weeks after the* Mona *disaster.*
(DAILY RECORD AND SUNDAY MAIL)

Applications to join a new crew had poured in, the first of them within hours of the disaster and the new coxswain was Jimmy 'Painter' Gall, the ex-trawlerman who had served as bowman of the *John Ryburn* in 1930. He had been second coxswain of the *Mona* under Jim Coull from 1935 and had seen war service on minesweeping trawlers. Second Coxswain Laurie Anderson's wartime experiences included having his ship blown up under him and spending two hours in the freezing Moray Firth before being picked up. After the war, he had spent four years on the South Georgia whale fishery. Alex 'Eck' Dorward DSC, the new bowman, had survived the blowing up of his minesweeper off Harwich in 1943. A temporary RNLI motor mechanic, Andy Mitchell, was also sent to the station.

Thirty-eight men had volunteered to form a new crew by the time the relief lifeboat City of Bradford II *arrived at Broughty Ferry on 22 December 1959.*
At front, from left; Coxswain Jimmy Gall, Second Coxswain Laurie Anderson, Bowman Alex Dorward, Rab Barclay, Alex Gall, Harper Robertson and Davie Laing. At rear; Head Launcher Charlie Knight, Willie Findlay, Dick Alexander and Jim Coull jun.
(DUNDEE ART GALLERIES AND MUSEUMS)

The maroons were fired for the first time after the disaster at 5.35 a.m. on 13 April 1960 following reports that a small vessel was firing distress flares off Newburgh in Fife. The *City of Bradford II* was launched into a full south-westerly gale seven minutes later and proceeded up river towards Newburgh. It was first thought that the vessel stranded off the Fife shore might be the small Dutch coaster *Ellen M* which was known to be making her way up to Perth on the high spring tide. The *Ellen M* had reached Perth safely and the stranded vessel turned out to be the Tay Sand Company's *Tay Buoy*. This was relayed to the lifeboat shortly before she lost radio contact due to the screening effect of the hills.

As Coxswain Gall took the lifeboat up river, his crew spotted another sand boat, the *Middlebank*, aground in Wormit Bay, one mile west of the Tay Bridge. The *Middlebank*'s skipper shouted that he was not in need of immediate assistance and the lifeboat carried on to the *Tay Buoy* which was found hard aground and leaking badly one mile west of Newburgh. She was in no immediate danger and Jimmy Gall agreed to call at Newburgh Pier to arrange for a pump to be sent out to her. The *City of Bradford II* was returning to station when she found that the *Middlebank* had freed herself but was now in a perilous position just 200 yards from the piers of the Tay Bridge and dragging her anchor.

The *Middlebank*'s crew at first suspected that the lifeboatmen had a claim for salvage in mind and refused the offer of a tow. It soon dawned on them, however, that they were in a dangerous position and two attempts were made to tow the sand boat to safety. On the first attempt, Andy Mitchell reported the lifeboat's engines were overheating. They were allowed to cool down before a second attempt was made to tow the sandboat off, this time stern first, but the *Middlebank*'s crew managed to wind the tow rope round their own propeller and the lifeboat had to cast off rather hurriedly to avoid being dragged into her stern. A tug was summoned from Dundee Harbour and the *City of Bradford II* was secured in Dundee Fish Dock until tide and sea conditions would allow her to be rehoused. Forty-five tins of petrol had to be brought to the dock by lorry and the boat refuelled before her weary crew could return home over 16 hours after the maroons were fired.

The City of Bradford II *alongside in Dundee Fish Dock on 14 April 1960 after the service to the sandboats* Tay Buoy *and* Middlebank. *Coxswain Jimmy Gall is facing the camera in sou'wester and Bowman Alex Dorward is standing aft.*
Jimmy Gall was awarded a parchment by the Royal Humane Society after he dived into Broughty Harbour and saved the life of a four year old boy in March 1935. Three years later, in May 1938, a six-year-old boy fell from the Broughty Pilot Pier and was swept under the low tide staging. Gall ran from Ambrose Street, dived straight in and pulled him to safety.
(DAILY RECORD AND SUNDAY MAIL)

The *City of Bradford II* was launched at 12.30 a.m. on 5 June 1960 when the cruiser *Margaret* was reported adrift in the river with six people aboard. The disabled cruiser was towed safely to the Fish Dock. Two days later she carried out a ten hour search for three students reported missing in a small boat. The boat was found completely shipshape near The Pool by the sand boat *Little Orme* and the bodies of the missing students were picked up in St Andrews Bay the following week.

The *City of Bradford II* was 30 years old and could only serve as a temporary replacement for the *Mona*. On 15 April 1960, the day after the *Tay Buoy* and *Middlebank* services, it was announced that the new Broughty Ferry lifeboat would be a 47 foot long Watson type with fully enclosed wheelhouse. She was powered by twin five cylinder, 60 horsepower Gardner diesels and was capable of 9 knots. Christened *The Robert,* she sailed north from Littlehampton crewed by RNLI staff and Coxswain Jimmy Gall, Motor Mechanic John Jack, Alex Dorward and Rab Barclay. The crew of the North Carr lightship manned the side to cheer her as she passed at 8.00 a.m. on Thursday, 17 November. Second Coxswain Laurie Anderson brought the *City of Bradford II* down to meet *The Robert* at the fairway buoy and the two lifeboats sailed in company to Broughty Ferry where two helicopters from RAF Leuchars flew low overhead and hundreds had lined the shore to greet the new boat.

Part of the enormous crowd that gathered in bright sunshine at Broughty Ferry on Monday, 15 May 1961 when The Robert *was named by the Duchess of Kent. The day was not without its share of incident. Shortly before the Duchess arrived, a fire engine had to be called after someone lit a large bonfire next to cars parked on the Pilot Pier. All eyes were drawn to the river a few minutes later when the motor mechanic of the Anstruther lifeboat, Donald Jack, had to commandeer a small boat and rescue three young men after a small catamaran capsized just off the harbour entrance. Later, it was found that someone had accidentally severed a cable and disabled the loudspeaker system with the result that the speeches were inaudible.*
(DUNDEE COURIER AND EVENING TELEGRAPH)

The Robert undertook her first service even before her naming ceremony when the Dutch MV *Tasman*, inbound for Newburgh to pick up a cargo of stone chips, went on the Abertay Sands on the evening of 18 January 1961. Honorary Secretary Andrew Young arrived at the boatshed in white tie and tails after being called out of a masonic function by the police. Watched by 200 cheering spectators who had raced to the boatshed on hearing the maroons, the lifeboat was launched into a force eight gale at 8.25 p.m. The coaster had given an inaccurate position and *The Robert* carried out a two hour search south towards the North Carr lightship before sighting the *Tasman* on the south side of the banks. She floated off on the rising tide at 2.30 a.m. and Jimmy Gall told her master to steer south-east into deep water.

The Dutchman clearly suspected that the lifeboatmen were about to claim salvage and, immediately he was clear of the banks, he doused all his lights. Unaware that the darkened *Tasman* was sneaking up river towards Buddon Ness, the lifeboat spent another 90 minutes searching for her in the heavy seas on the banks. Loud wireless appeals from the coaster for a pilot brought this absurd game of hide and seek to an end and *The Robert* returned to station at 6.00 a.m.

The Broughty Ferry lifeboatmen's festive celebrations at the end of 1961 were interrupted twice. The first launch took place at 7.30 p.m. on Christmas Day after flares were reported over St Andrews Bay. It was a bitterly cold night and spray turned to ice immediately it landed on deck. A search revealed nothing and *The Robert* was secured alongside the Pilot Pier at midnight. The maroons were fired again at 7.15 p.m. on New Year's Day and the lifeboat took a doctor out to attend an injured man aboard the Abertay lightship.

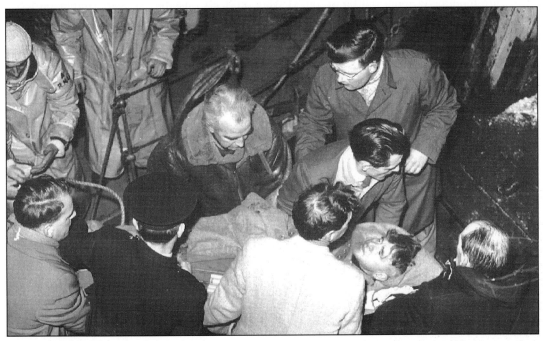

On New Year's Day, 1962, Jim Mathieson, one of the crew of the Abertay lightship, slipped on her ice-covered deck and plunged 15 feet down a hatch. The Robert *was launched with Dr John Simpson on board and landed the injured seaman to a waiting ambulance at 8.00 p.m.*
(DUNDEE COURIER AND EVENING TELEGRAPH)

The late 1950s and early 1960s brought a number of innovations to Broughty Ferry lifeboat station. The first flight of air-sea rescue helicopters had been established at Leuchars in 1955. With the helicopters had come VHF radio telephony, at first intended purely for close range co-ordination with the RAF, but soon to become the main method of voice communication between lifeboats and the shore. Other innovations included diesel engines, single-lever engine controls that freed the mechanic and second mechanic for other tasks, the echo-sounder, radar, the radio direction finder and the Decca Navigator. The crew was also changing with an increasing number being drawn from among the membership of the Royal Tay Yacht Club and from those with backgrounds in the Merchant Navy, the Royal Navy and the Police.

The very nature of lifeboat work was also going through a period of fundamental change. Gone were the days when fishing boats and sailing traders plied the Tay. Cargo vessels were no longer 250 ton sailing barques, nor even 5,000 ton steamers; huge bulk carriers and tankers weighing in at 90,000 tons were already coming out of Japanese shipyards and even larger vessels were planned. Put simply, fewer, bigger, better equipped ships meant that fewer commercial vessels were being lost. From the 1950s onwards, however, the explosion in leisure sailing meant that, as yachtsmen were increasingly numbered among the crew, so an ever-increasing number of calls on the lifeboat were from pleasure sailors.

One of the most fundamental innovations in Broughty Ferry lifeboat station's history took to the waters of the Tay on the afternoon of Wednesday, 22 April 1964 as Scotland's first inflatable inshore lifeboat set out on her trials. At the helm was the station's new full-time coxswain, Alick Mackay, formerly the motor mechanic of the Arbroath lifeboat. The new inshore lifeboat was named *Pinafore* as it had been partly funded from the proceeds of the

1964 production of *HMS Pinafore* by the Edinburgh University Savoy Opera Group. Her first service launch came just five days after her trials, at 1.26 p.m. on 27 April, when a man was reported missing from the construction works on the new Tay Road Bridge. Impressing all concerned with her speed and manoeuvrability, the inshore lifeboat crewed by Alick Mackay and Motor Mechanic John Jack carried out two searches but the missing man was not found.

The speed of response of the inshore boat was amply demonstrated at the end of the following month. At about 4.30 a.m. on 31 May, Police Constable Stewart Hutchison woke Alick Mackay to tell him that a man could be seen in difficulties in the river about 300 yards off Broughty Castle. John Jack was roused and the inshore boat was under way in about three minutes. Within eight minutes, the 'man', who turned out to be a boy of about 15, was picked up and brought ashore. The boy said that he was from Newport and had fallen overboard while out fishing. Only after he had been given dry clothing, a hot drink, and delivered to Newport, did it transpire that the young man was on the run from Rossie Farm Approved School near Montrose!

Willie Pyke and Graham May return to station with ILB No. 173, which was on station at Broughty Ferry from 1971 to 1983.
(DAVID ANGUS)

The building of the Tay Road Bridge was a massive undertaking and not without its hazards. *The Robert* landed two men after one of the bridge contractor's safety boats broke down in November 1964. Both *The Robert* and the inshore boat were involved in an early morning search for a workman who fell from the bridge works on 13 March 1965 and *The Robert* stood by when a ship fouled the new bridge in October 1965. The inshore boat and *The Robert* were both launched shortly before 10.00 p.m. on 11 November 1965 when a section of the roadway fell onto a temporary structure below, sending a large crane and two diesel bogies crashing into the deepest part of the river. Nothing was found and three men were later reported drowned. Crewing the inshore boat on this service were Coxswain Alick Mackay and his 18 year-old son Alasdair.

RNLB *The Robert*
(DUNDEE COURIER AND EVENING TELEGRAPH)

By 1969, the inshore lifeboat, the offshore boat and the Leuchars based helicopters were operating effectively as a team. On the evening of 21 September that year, the relief offshore lifeboat *W & S* and the inshore lifeboat were launched after distress flares were seen off the mouth of the river. A strong south-westerly gale had sprung up and gusts of 71 mph were recorded at RAF Leuchars. John Jack and Hugh Scott in the inshore lifeboat found the yacht *Fun and Games* in trouble off Monifieth, took three men off her and landed them on a nearby sandbank. A 202 Squadron helicopter piloted by Flying Officer Paul Shaw had also seen the flares while returning from another distress call off Crail. Shaw picked the three men up from the sandbank and landed them at Monifieth.

At the mouth of the river, Jack and Scott found the 38 foot yacht *Seagrim* in difficulties on The Bar. The inshore boat landed five of her crew at Monifieth. The three men remaining on the yacht took her into sheltered water at Buddon escorted by the *W & S*. The helicopter, meanwhile, responded to reports of a trimaran, the *Nimble Iki,* in apparent difficulties off Tentsmuir. The trimaran did not require assistance and, lacking a radio, her crew had to resort to an old-fashioned two-fingered gesture to signal to the helicopter crew that their services were not needed.

Some years earlier, in 1964, the *Nimble-Iki* was being delivered to the Tay by Second Coxswain Laurie Anderson and former crewman Willie Findlay when she got into difficulties in St Andrews Bay. *The Robert* towed the *Nimble Iki* into Broughty Ferry and branch chairman Captain William Keay rang the trimaran's owner, his great-nephew Ron Bonar, to suggest that a donation to branch funds might be in order. Ron Bonar has since succeeded to the post of branch chairman.

The former Cromarty lifeboat *Lilla Marras, Douglas and Will,* was on temporary duty at Broughty Ferry when she was launched at 9.35 p.m. on Saturday, 28 August 1976 after a cabin cruiser was reported in trouble near the Bell Rock in rough seas and a force 6 wind. Nothing was found and the lifeboat returned to station after five hours at sea on what turned out to be a hoax call. Later that same weekend, the *Lilla Marras* stood by the 17,000 ton liner *Uganda* after a pilotage error set her aground on the Abertay Sands. Stuck fast for over 12 hours, the *Uganda* was refloated on the tide with the help of three oil rig supply vessels. While returning to station, the lifeboat gave assistance to the disabled motor cruiser *Hillary Anne*.

The crew of The Robert *in April 1969. Front, from left: Hugh Scott, Davie Laing, Coxswain Alick Mackay, Harper Robertson, Motor Mechanic John Jack and Willie Findlay. At rear: Ron Alstaff, Willie Miller, Honorary Secretary Jim Potter, Alisdair Mackay, John Brewster, Alistair Piggot, Rab Barclay and Angus Munro. John Jack succeeded Alick Mackay as coxswain, a position he held until 1989. Coxswain Jack's lifeboat service was recognised with the award, in 1986, of the British Empire Medal.*
(DUNDEE COURIER AND EVENING TELEGRAPH)

The pilot of a Piper Commanche light aircraft became disorientated in fog and crashed into the Tay on the afternoon of Sunday, 5 February 1978. Birdwatchers raised the alarm and the inshore lifeboat was launched. Graham May and Frank Donnelly reached the scene within ten minutes to find two men and a 15 year-old boy clinging to the nosewheel of the wrecked aircraft. One man had a head wound and all three were suffering from shock and exposure after 20 minutes in water just five degrees above freezing point.

The presence of the three oil rig supply vessels at the refloating of the *Uganda* signalled another fundamental change in the history of the river. Jute, Dundee's great staple industry, had been in decline since the early years of the century and the city was littered with decaying, abandoned mills. New industries attracted to the city in the post-war years were only part of the answer and the North Sea oil industry was seen as the means of Dundee's economic salvation.

New lifeboats were also being developed to meet new challenges. Among the new designs was the 52 foot Arun class self-righting lifeboat fitted with twin 460 horsepower Caterpillar diesel engines and capable of 18 knots. As the prototype Arun began trials in 1969, the Longhope lifeboat *TGB* was lost along with her entire crew of eight. Just ten months later, in January 1970, the Fraserburgh lifeboat *Duchess of Kent* capsized and all but one of her crew drowned. These disasters stirred up a hornet's nest of controversy, much of it based on ill-informed press coverage that accused the RNLI of sending lifeboatmen to sea in out-dated and unsafe boats. Some newspapers recalled the *Mona* disaster and focused on Broughty Ferry lifeboat station but, as Honorary Secretary Jim Potter told one newspaper, the Broughty Ferry crew were entirely happy with *The Robert* and had full confidence in her.

A new boat was, however, required and the Broughty Ferry crew chose to follow their Aberdeen colleagues in opting for an Arun class at a cost of £220,000. Led by Branch President Ian Low, a massive fund raising effort began towards the end of 1975 and, by October 1976, £104,000 had been raised from direct approaches to public bodies, companies and trusts. Over £126,000 had been collected by March 1977 when the RNLI announced that Arun number 1056 had been allocated to Broughty Ferry and a public appeal for the balance of £94,000 was launched.

Marks and Spencer's contributed £1,000, the Dundee Students Charities Campaign raised money to pay for the new boat's electronics, £50 came in from station personnel at RAF Leuchars and other donations were presented by women's guilds, masonic lodges, round tables, Carnoustie Townswomen's Guild, Broughty Ferry Traders Association and the Glasgow Angus Society, to name but a few. One group of schoolchildren decided to hold a jumble sale in aid of the appeal and inadvertently called at the home of Coxswain John Jack.

Followed by Dundee Branch Chairman Captain Colin Keay, President of the RNLI the Duke of Kent takes his leave at the end of the naming and dedication ceremony for the Spirit of Tayside *on Monday, 17 July 1978. Second Coxswain Hugh Scott and Motor Mechanic Willie Pyke look on.*
(CHRISTOPHER BONAR)

The new lifeboat arrived on 6 May 1978 and was named *Spirit of Tayside* at a ceremony in Broughty Harbour on Monday, 17 July. *Spirit of Tayside* undertook her first service on 3 September 1978 when she towed a small motor launch to safety. Her baptism of fire, however, came that Christmas Eve after the coaster *Fendyke* found herself in difficulties in a force 10 gale. Captain Ron Dennis decided to run for shelter in the Tay and was approaching The Bar when his ship was struck by a giant wave that sent water cascading down the funnel into her engine room. The electricity supply was shorted out, the steering gear was disabled and water got into her accommodation and flooded cabins. On the bridge, Captain Dennis was thrown first one way, then the other, breaking both his arms and injuring a leg.

The oil rig support vessel *Stena Piper* saw the *Fendyke's* distress flares and reported the coaster drifting towards Buddon Ness and in desperate trouble. The *Spirit of Tayside* was launched from Broughty Ferry and a Wessex air-sea rescue helicopter was scrambled from Leuchars. The coaster was rolling through 60 degrees in 40 foot seas but the helicopter pilot handled his aircraft with consummate skill as his crew lifted the injured Captain Dennis off and took him straight to hospital in Dundee. The helicopter returned to the *Fendyke* and took off Nellie Watson, the 55 year-old wife of the Chief Engineer, before going back to Leuchars to refuel. A second Wessex then approached the coaster and Flight Sergeant Evans was being winched down onto her deck when he was struck by one of the ship's aerials and badly stunned. He was taken back up into the aircraft and a larger Sea King helicopter was summoned to take off the six men still aboard the *Fendyke*.

The *Spirit of Tayside* was also trying to reach the *Fendyke* but the combination of an easterly gale and a strong ebb tide had caused huge waves on the Tay Bar. Second Coxswain Hugh Scott takes up the story;

While crossing The Bar, the lifeboat encountered three or four enormous seas, two of which threw her on her beam ends. The second of these seas caused the engine cut-outs to operate. These are designed to come on at about 110 degrees of heel. The same sea washed the searchlight off the port wing of the flying bridge. The engines were restarted once the boat had regained an even keel and we proceeded only to find a much larger sea approaching, whereupon the engines were increased to full power to climb up this sea. On breaking through the top, the boat fell into a hole and landed on her port side. Four of the crew were injured.

Coxswain Jack and myself were on the flying bridge negotiating these enormous, irregular seas and navigating down the channel as there were no navigation buoys lit. When we landed at the bottom of the hole, both he and I received injuries, myself with a broken ankle and the coxswain with torn knee ligaments

Despite his broken ankle, Hugh Scott took the wheel as John Jack limped below to check on his crew. Second Mechanic Willie Findlay had torn ligaments and all had suffered cuts and bruises but of Angus Munro there was no sign. It was immediately assumed that he had been washed over the side and a helicopter was alerted to search for him. Moments later, the *Spirit of Tayside* was again hurled onto her side and the engine cut-outs operated once more, a desperately dangerous situation in such close proximity to the sandbanks. Motor Mechanic Willie Pyke took the wheel and, once the engines were restarted for a second time, kept one hand close to the cut-out switches until the lifeboat was out of immediate danger.

Abandoned by her crew, the disabled coaster Fendyke *was driven ashore on Buddon Sands from where she was later salvaged.*
(DUNDEE COURIER AND EVENING TELEGRAPH)

Eventually, a shaken Angus Munro emerged from the forward cabin. It transpired that he had just left the heads, after relieving an urgent call of nature, when the *Spirit of Tayside* was hit by the huge seas. As the boat crashed down onto her port side, he was flung across the cabin and knocked unconscious. Angus recalls climbing up to the wheelhouse where he found injured crewmen groaning in agony and loose gear rolling about the deck amid puddles of sea water that had jetted in through one of the side windows. The lifeboat's navigation aids had all failed and, in an attempt to fix her position, John Jack limped out onto the heaving after deck to fire a flare on which, it was hoped, the coastguard station at Fife Ness could take a bearing.

The morning of Friday, 13 May 1988, was notably unlucky for the crew of the tug Defiant *which ran onto the Gaa Sands while inbound from the Forth. There was insufficient water on the banks for the* Spirit of Tayside *to close the stranded tug and a Wessex air-sea resuce helicopter was scrambled from RAF Leuchars. Two of the tug's crew were transferred to the lifeboat and one was landed at Buddon Ness from where he was taken to hospital by ambulance. The tug was refloated on the tide and towed up river to Dundee by the lifeboat. Sadly, this was one of the last services carried out by lifeboat together with the Leuchars-based helicopters. Despite a vigorous public campaign in favour of its retention, the RAF search and rescue squadron was withdrawn in 1993 as part of the defence cuts.*
(ROYAL NATIONAL LIFEBOAT INSTITUTION)

The *Fendyke* was already ashore on Buddon Sands, her crew safe at Leuchars, when the lifeboat cleared the river. Recrossing The Bar to return to station was out of the question so, in company with the Arbroath lifeboat *Duke of Montrose*, the *Spirit of Tayside* sailed south through the storm to Leith. Once her injured crewmen had been despatched to Edinburgh Royal Infirmary, the rest sat in thoughtful silence in the after cabin, each of them clutching a glass of brandy.

The *Spirit of Tayside's* storm damage was repaired and Acting Coxswain Bill Ireland took the lifeboat out of Leith at 3.00 p.m. on 2 January 1979 to return to Broughty Ferry. The lifeboat was just about to clear the pierheads when the harbourmaster yelled across that a fishing boat was in trouble. Forth Coastguard confirmed the harbourmaster's message and directed the lifeboat to a position 11 miles south-east of the Isle of May where the St Monans registered *Paragon* had developed a serious leak. Willie Pyke and Willie Findlay were put aboard the *Paragon* with a portable pump and the fishing boat was escorted back to her home port.

The lifeboat resumed her passage home and Acting Coxswain Ireland was turning into the Tay when he heard that the pilot cutter *Newcraig* had suffered engine failure. *Spirit of Tayside* rounded off what had been an eventful festive season by taking the *Newcraig* in tow to the Fish Dock. The inshore lifeboat had also been on service that afternoon when two boys were reported adrift on an ice floe off Kingoodie. The ILB was trapped in the ice for some minutes but the boys were landed safely.

Broughty Ferry lifeboats are regularly called out to recover people who have committed suicide by jumping from the Tay Road Bridge. Picking up a body is always distressing but, on two occasions, the lifeboats have been on hand to save life. One such service began when a woman motorist reported a man clinging to the railings of the bridge at 11.20 p.m. on 18 January 1985. The Arun class lifeboat *Newsbuoy* was launched and, when the man did jump shortly before 1.00 a.m. the following morning, he was picked up almost immediately and put ashore to a waiting ambulance at Camperdown Lockway. The crews of both the inshore and offshore boats saw in the New Year of 1993 responding to another such call.

RNLB Spirit of Tayside
(JOHN JACK)

The *Newsbuoy* was on relief duty at Broughty Ferry from October 1984 as the *Spirit of Tayside* was undergoing an extended refit at Herd and Mackenzie's Buckie shipyard. Among the many modifications undertaken were the addition of adjustable trim tabs designed to improve the boat's sea-keeping qualities. New navigation aids were fitted and the derrick formerly used to launch the small inshore lifeboat carried on the superstructure was replaced by a folding slipway. At the beginning of April 1985, three days after *Spirit of Tayside* returned to Broughty Ferry, she escorted the semi-submersible *Happy Mariner* bringing Captain Scott's polar exploration ship RRS *Discovery* back to the city of her birth.

On the morning of 30 July 1995, as the rest of Scotland basked in a summer heatwave, a thick, grey haar blanketed the Tay estuary. For the Broughty Ferry lifeboatmen and their families, the relaxed calm of a summer Sunday was rudely shattered by the insistent bleeping of electronic pagers. Three long signals followed by three short ones indicated a 'shout' for

Four month old Ross Munro was christened aboard the Spirit of Tayside *on 29 August 1993. Front, from left: Rev Dr John Cameron, Godmother Fiona Sellers, Ross and his parents Alison and Lee Munro. At rear; Dave Martin, Liam Sullivan, Bob Jeffrey and Neil Gall.*

The lifeboat service has always been very much a family affair. To date, Lee Munro, his father Angus and his brother David have accumulated 51 years of service. Neil Gall was but the latest Broughty Ferry lifeboatman to bear that name which has an illustrious history of lifeboat service stretching back to the first Buddon Ness boat in the 1830s.

Gavin Philp, the son of crewman Ian Philp and his wife Wendy, was christened on the Spirit of Tayside *in June 1995. Gavin's distant relative, Captain Robert Philp, was a member of the crew on the first trial of the* Cork Lifeboat *at St Andrews in January 1802.*

(DUNDEE COURIER AND EVENING TELEGRAPH)

Broughty Ferry offshore and inshore lifeboat crews, January 1996. Standing from left: Robert McTavish, Coxswain Jim Hughan, Second Coxswain Willie Pyke, Neil Rodger, Ian Philp, Second Mechanic Dave Martin, Ali Mathers, Pete Hay, Murray Brown, Launcher Sid Keiller, Liam Sullivan, Honorary Medical Adviser Dr Maureen Wilkinson, Deputy Coxswain Brian Summers, Andrew Jeffrey, Emergency Mechanic Bob Jeffrey, Andy Stevenson and Ian Reid. At front, Lee Munro and Colin Scott.

(ROBERT BROWN)

both the inshore and offshore boats. The planned sailing trip, the run in the car, the leisurely Sunday lunch, all were instantly abandoned as the lifeboatmen raced to the boatshed.

A cabin cruiser with four men on board had been reported missing after leaving Newburgh the previous afternoon bound for Arbroath. The relief inshore lifeboat *Pride of Nuneaton and Bedworth* was launched within three minutes of the alert and, moments later, the relief Arun class *Edith Emilie* slipped her moorings and thundered off into the mist.

Helmsman Murray Brown and the crew of the inshore lifeboat began a search up river towards Newburgh. Coxswain Jim Hughan took the *Edith Emilie* down river to the banks. Suddenly, at 1.30 p.m., as the *Edith Emilie* passed down the line of the Gaa Sands, lookouts yelled, 'Man in the water, port side!' A shaft of sunlight had illuminated a lone figure in a patch of debris. Jim Hughan took the lifeboat into the shallows and crewman Ian Philp leapt into the sea to support the survivor until he could be lifted aboard.

The Arbroath lifeboat *Inchcape* joined the search as the *Edith Emilie* hastened back to Broughty Ferry and a waiting ambulance. The Anstruther lifeboat *Kingdom of Fife* was making her best speed to the scene, the inshore lifeboat was speeding down river and an air-sea rescue helicopter was circling low overhead. Coastguards were combing beaches from Tentsmuir to Carnoustie. Then a yachtsman reported the grim discovery of a body lashed to a drum west of Buddon Ness and the Arbroath lifeboat was directed to her position. The *Inchcape*'s crew recovered this body, along with another found underneath the drum, and landed them at Broughty Ferry.

Visibility deteriorated to less than 100 yards as the four lifeboats continued the search for the remaining missing man. Anstruther lifeboat found a yacht in a dangerous position in thick fog south of the Abertay Sands and it was towed up river to Tayport. The *Inchcape* and the *Kingdom of Fife* were stood down in the early evening and the Broughty Ferry inshore lifeboat crew returned to station after more than seven hours in their small, uncomfortable craft. Within minutes of being rehoused, the *Pride of Nuneaton and Bedworth* was refuelled and ready for immediate service.

RNLB *Edith Emilie* returned to Broughty Ferry as evening shadows lengthened over the village. The wives waiting anxiously by the boatshed, the lights in the windows of the old cottages, the comforting bulk of the castle and the darkening outline of the Scaup Beacon, a setting familiar to generations of returning lifeboatmen, lay before her as she edged towards her mooring.

The volunteer lifeboatmen of Broughty Ferry, Tayport, Buddon Ness, St Andrews, Boarhills and Fife Ness have saved more than 800 lives since John Honey made his courageous dash into the breakers at the East Sands on that January afternoon in 1800. Their story is one of continuing selfless endeavour in the face of often terrible odds, even tragedy. Yet, in a supposedly cynical age, lifeboat crews are not a breed apart. They are just ordinary men and women driven to their hazardous duty by the same altruistic impulse that inspired Sir William Hillary to found the RNLI for the preservation of life from shipwreck.

Today's lifeboat crews might enjoy all the benefits of fast, modern boats and the very latest in sophisticated equipment, but the sea has not changed. It is still the same fickle, grimly determined adversary faced by the crew of the *Cork Lifeboat;* by the men who rowed the *Mary Hartley* over the banks to the *Dalhousie;* by the crew of the *English Mechanic* as they battled through the blizzard to the *Neils;* by Jamie Gourlay's crew as they struggled off the beach at Boarhills to the *Fransis;* by the crew of the *John and Sarah Hatfield* as they pulled alongside the *Prinses Wilhelmina;* by Charles Gall's crew as they grappled the *Maria* alongside the *Daydream* and, above all, by the men of the *Mona.*

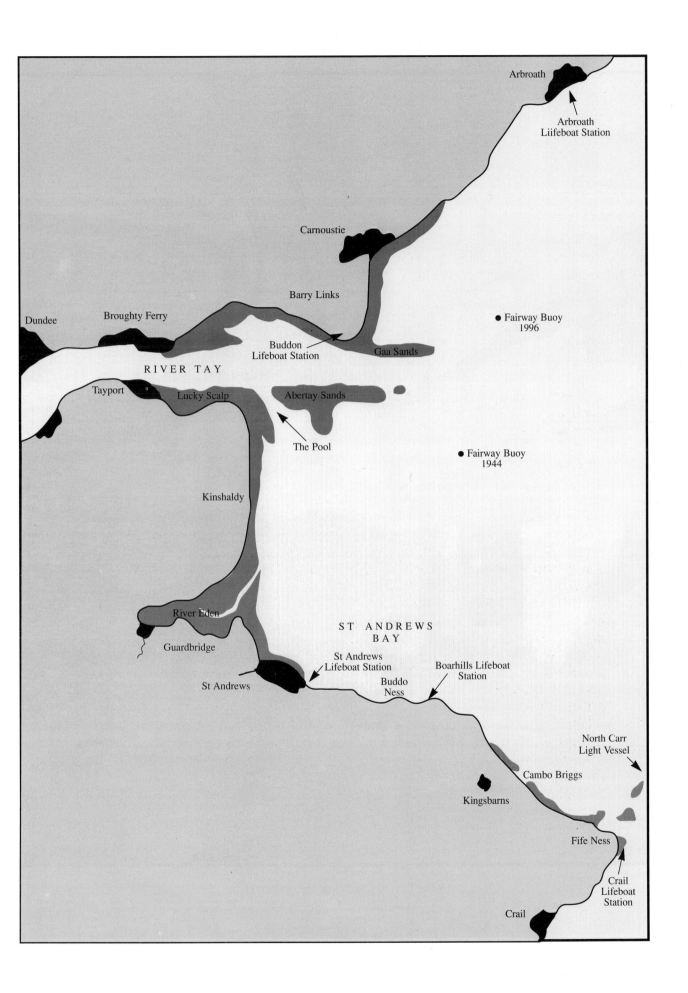

Arbroath

Arbroath
Liifeboat Station

Carnoustie

Barry Links

Dundee

Broughty Ferry

Buddon
Lifeboat Station

Gaa Sands

Fairway Buoy
1996

RIVER TAY

Tayport

Lucky Scalp

Abertay Sands

The Pool

Fairway Buoy
1944

Kinshaldy

River Eden

ST ANDREWS
BAY

Guardbridge

St Andrews
Lifeboat Station

Boarhills Lifeboat
Station

St Andrews

Buddo
Ness

North Carr
Light Vessel

Cambo Briggs

Kingsbarns

Fife Ness

Crail
Lifeboat
Station

Crail

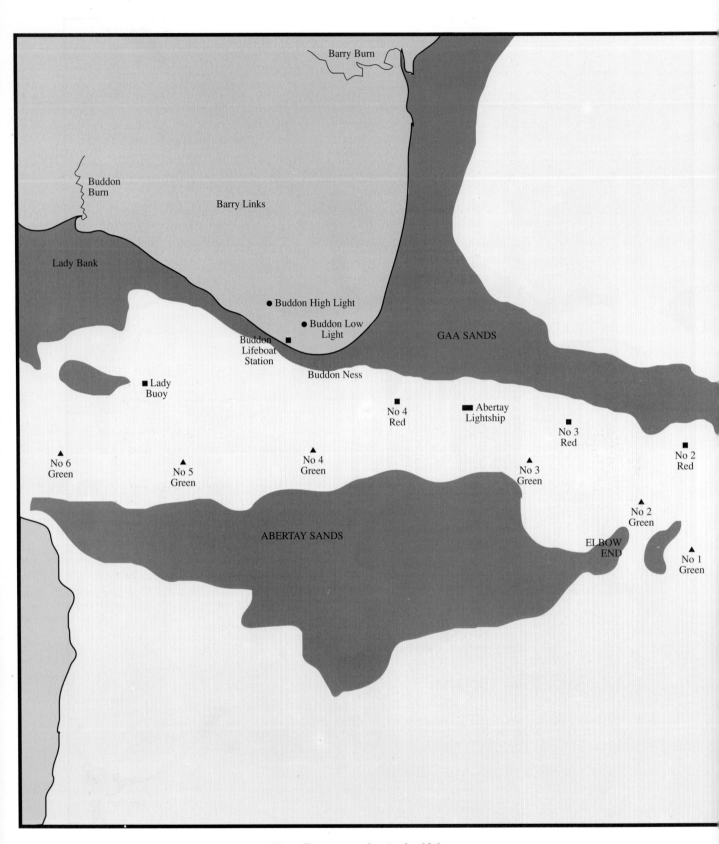

River Tay approaches in the 19th century

Acknowledgements

It would be quite impossible to name everyone who has contributed to this book. To those inadequately acknowledged, my apologies as well as my thanks.

Dundee City Archives Department were, as ever, courteous and helpful, as were Dundee University Library Archives and Manuscripts Department and Dundee Museums and Art Galleries. The Local History Department of Dundee Central Library, Broughty Ferry Branch Library and, in Angus, Carnoustie and Arbroath Libraries all lent valuable assistance.

In St Andrews, I am indebted to the St Andrews University Library Department of Archives and Manuscripts, the St Andrews University Scottish Institute of Maritime Studies, the Hay Fleming Library and St Andrews Preservation Trust Museum.

The considerable storehouse of information held by the National Library of Scotland in Edinburgh was a valuable source, as were the City of Edinburgh Central Library, Perth and Cupar Libraries. I must also acknowledge the contributions of the Rescue Records and Public Relations Departments of the Royal National Lifeboat Institution, HM Coastguard, the City of Aberdeen Arts and Museums Services, *The Press and Journal*, the Northern Lighthouse Board, Radio Tay, the William MacGonagall Appreciation Society, Perth Museum, Tayside Police Museum and Crail Museum.

A particular debt of gratitude is due to D.C. Thomson & Co. Ltd. Without their assistance so generously given, this project would have been very much the poorer.

In addition, many people kindly allowed me access to their memories and private collections including Jeff Morris and Iain Buik of the Lifeboat Enthusiasts Society, Bob Baird, Maureen Bell (nee Grieve), Brian Callison, Bill Flett, George Ritchie, Vina Robertson (nee Grieve) and George Rosie. Among the lifeboat crew and former crew who added first hand recollections were Coxswain James Hughan, ex-Coxswain John Jack BEM, Second Coxswain Willie Pyke, Rab Barclay, Murray Brown, Frank Donnelly, Davie Laing, Dave Martin, Angus Munro, Lee Munro, Liam Sullivan and Alex Watson.

My thanks also to Dundee Branch Chairman Ron Bonar, Christopher Bonar, Captain George Dobbie, Susan Hughan for her artwork, Bob Brown, David Angus, Colin Wight and PBM (Commercial) Photographic for photographs and PBM Photographic Support Services for hand printing, Ron Milne for the charts and Wilma Milne who read and corrected the proofs.

Andrew Jeffrey, Broughty Ferry, 1996.

Bibliography

Arbroath Guide, The.

Arbroath Herald, The.

Broughty Ferry Guide and Carnoustie Gazette, The.

Bruce, George. *Wrecks and Reminiscences of St Andrews Bay with the History of the Lifeboat.* John Leng & Co., Dundee, 1884.

Coast Burghs Observer, The.

Dawson, Major A.J. *Britain's Life-boats.* Hodder & Stoughton, London, 1923.

Dibdin, Charles. *Royal National Life-boat Institution: Its Origin and History.* Wm. Clowes, London 1901.

Dundee Advertiser, The.

Dundee Branch, RNLI, *Returns of Service for Broughty Ferry Lifeboat Station, 1862-1995.*

Dundee Chronicle, The.

Dundee Courier, The.

Dundee Harbour Commission. *Records lodged with Dundee University Library Archives and Manuscripts Department*

Dundee Harbour Trust. *Records lodged with Dundee District Council Archives Department.*

East Fife Observer, The.

East Fife Record, The.

Farr, A.D. *Let Not The Deep. The Story of the Royal National Lifeboat Institution.* Impulse Books, Aberdeen 1982

Fifeshire Journal, The.

Fraternity of Masters and Seamen, Trinity House, Dundee. *Records lodged with Dundee District Council Archives Department.*

Hillary, Sir William. *Appeal to the British Nation on the Humanity and Policy of forming a National Institution for the Preservation of Lives and Property from Shipwreck.* G.B. Whittaker, London, 1823.

Howarth, P.J.F. *The Life-boat Story.* Routledge & Keegan Paul, London, 1957.

Howie, Gillian. *The Story of Arbroath Lifeboat.* Arbroath, 1982.

Lamb, Sir John. *The Life-boat and its Work.* Clowes, London, 1911.

Lewis, Richard. *History of the Life-boat and its Work.* Macmillan, London, 1874.

Lifeboat, The. Journal of the RNLI. From Issue No.1, March 1852.

Naval Officer in Charge, Dundee, 1939 to 1945. *Records held by the Public Record Office, London.*

Northern Warder, The.

Ritchie, George F. *The Real Price of Fish. Aberdeen Steam Trawler Losses 1887-1961.* Hutton Press, Beverley, 1991.

Salmond J.B. *The Story of the R&A.* Macmillan & Co Ltd., London, 1956.

St Andrews Citizen, The.

Tragedy of the Mona, The. Radio Tay Programme, 1984.

Welch, Michael. *Anstruther Lifeboat Station. A History 1865-1985.* Anstruther, 1985.

Index